DE/CIPHER

First published in Great Britain in 2017 by Modern Books
An imprint of Elwin Street Productions Limited
14 Clerkenwell Green
London EC1R 0DP
www.modern-books.com

ISBN 978-1-911130-37-6

10 9 8 7 6 5 4 3 2 1

Printed in China

DE/CIPHER

THE GREATEST CODES EVER INVENTED
AND HOW TO BREAK THEM

MARK FRARY

CONTENTS

FOREWORD

Dr Stephen Bax

Like moths to a flame, human beings have been drawn irresistibly towards all kinds of mysteries and puzzles. So much do we relish them that we even invent fictional mysteries for detectives such as Sherlock Holmes to solve. Indeed, such is our fascination in particular for 'secret codes' and puzzles that we create an Indiana Jones to combine into a single hero our love of adventure, dashing athleticism and linguistic ingenuity, not to mention stylish hats.

But why invent fictional puzzles and codes when – as this inspiring and comprehensive volume testifies – the real world already offers us a host of intriguing genuine ciphers and codes to delight and frustrate us? In my own case, my work on cracking the mysterious Voynich manuscript (see opposite, and page 41) sprang directly from a boyhood fascination with all kinds of real-life codebreaking and decipherment, ancient and modern, including the mystery of hieroglyphs, the Rosetta Stone, runes and the Linear B of Crete. To add to the mysteries themselves, the characters involved in each story were often more eccentric and innovative than any Indiana Jones, as they worked against the odds to crack their particular codes.

When I was asked to introduce this book, and read through its packed pages, I was transported back once again into old worlds of adventure through which I had travelled before, visiting favourites such as the undeciphered Phaistos Disk or the wonderful Rongorongo script. Although these were old friends, I learned something fresh about them on every page. Who knew, for example, that Morse was a portrait painter inspired to work on his Morse code because of the death of his wife?

In addition, a host of lesser-known codes and ciphers, no less intriguing and fascinating, are set before us. These for me are new friends, so to speak – mysterious ancient ciphers, commercial codes, poetic codes, advanced encryption techniques, and much more besides. At the same time, we are introduced to a new cast of strange and delightful characters – encoders and decoders, soldiers and tricksters, charlatans and scientists, page after page of riddles and riddlers. Some of the mysteries are already solved, but many others still tantalize us, stubbornly resisting decipherment. So, for the old friends

The Voynich Manuscript, above, is one of many fascinating historical documents where codes and ciphers were used to conceal the contents from enemy eyes.

revisited, and the delightful new friends introduced, I offer the author my personal vote of gratitude.

Cracking any code calls for flexibility, dedication and hard work. But above all it calls for curiosity and a love of the new, to suspend our preconceptions and think outside the box of the conventional. That is why this book is a source of delight and inspiration, as well as of endless interest and insight. It calls to our curiosity and speaks to a basic human characteristic in us all: the passionate desire to explain and understand the unexplained and mysterious, and to enjoy the journey as we do so.

THE COMPLEXITY OF CRYPTOGRAPHY

In this book, we take a historical journey, starting from the very origins of cryptography in the Indus Valley some 5,000 to 6,000 years ago, and exploring the ways that the ancient Greeks and Egyptians used to keep their correspondence secret. From fifth-century BCE Greek historian Herodotus we learn not only of the events of daily life, but also many fascinating details, including a method of sending secret messages by tattooing the shaved heads of slaves – deployed by the tyrant Histiaeus, of the city of Miletus, in war against the Persians, and related in *Histories*. Once the hair grew, the messages were concealed. From Herodotus's account we are told that Histiaeus dispatched a messenger with the following instruction: 'When thou art come to Miletus, bid Aristagoras [Histiaeus's nephew] shave thy head, and look thereon'.

Herodotus also revealed another technique used by the Greeks – that of inscribing a message on a wooden tablet and covering the tablet in melted wax to hide it. These methods became known as steganography (from the Greek words *steganos,* meaning concealed, and *graphia,* meaning writing), and also include using invisible inks, hiding messages under postage stamps or placing dots under specific letters indicating that only those are to be read.

As Europe entered the Middle Ages, Arabic scholars emerged as the leading lights of the cryptological craft. Iraqi philosopher al-Kindi effectively created the profession of cryptanalysis or codebreaking with his invention of frequency analysis. His work was the starting gun for an epic race between cryptographers and cryptanalysts that continues to this day. European thinkers developed fiendish new techniques that used multiple alphabets to neuter frequency analysis and came up with the key to make codebreaking impossible . . . or so they thought. Yet in the ninetheeth century German cryptographer Friedrich Kasiski showed that even these supposedly impregnable techniques had their flaws.

By the early nineteenth century, the Industrial Revolution, greater international trade and the rise of telegraphy increased the need for secure communication at a distance. Samuel Morse gave the world his eponymous code while others recognized the need to go beyond this to make those communications secure. In the early twentieth century, as the world went to war, the stakes involved in the battle between codemakers and codebreakers were high. French soldier and codebreaking genius Georges Painvin helped thwart Germany's Spring Offensive, while the United States Army's Choctaw codetalkers ensured the Allies' communications were kept secret. The years between the world wars marked a significant turning point in cryptology – it was the end of the era in which encryption was carried out by hand and the start of the machine era, which enabled warring sides to convolute their messages with incredible complexity.

Yet even these ciphers were not immune to attack. The work of codebreakers at Bletchley Park in Britain was unknown to the public until many decades after the Second World War, but war leader Winston Churchill famously said that the conflict was shortened by a year because of the work carried out there. Mathematicians were by now the leading forces and their search for ever more complicated algorithms to conceal messages led directly to the beginning of the computer age. And the increasing complexity of information technology has dominated the world of cryptography ever since.

The difference between codes and ciphers

Although we tend to use the word 'cipher' interchangeably with the word 'code,' there are actually some important differences between them.

In essence, the distinction is as follows. Ciphers are systems for disguising the meaning of a message by replacing each of the individual letters in the message with other symbols. Codes, on the other hand, place more emphasis on meanings than characters, and tend to replace whole words or phrases according to a list contained in a codebook (a document or book used for gathering, storing and recording codes).

As a result, codes are more static and inflexible than ciphers. For example, a code might specify that the group of numbers '5487' replaces the word 'attack'. The means that any time 'attack' is written in a message, the encoded version will include the code group '5487'. Even if a codebook includes several options for encoding 'attack', the number of variations will be limited.

By contrast, when using a cipher, 'attack' might be encrypted in completely different ways in different parts of the same message, making it harder to spot the pattern. *Codes* helps to put the beguiling world of codes and ciphers into historical context but also provides the practical tools that anyone with a keen interest in the art and science of cryptology can use to break coded and encrypted messages themselves.

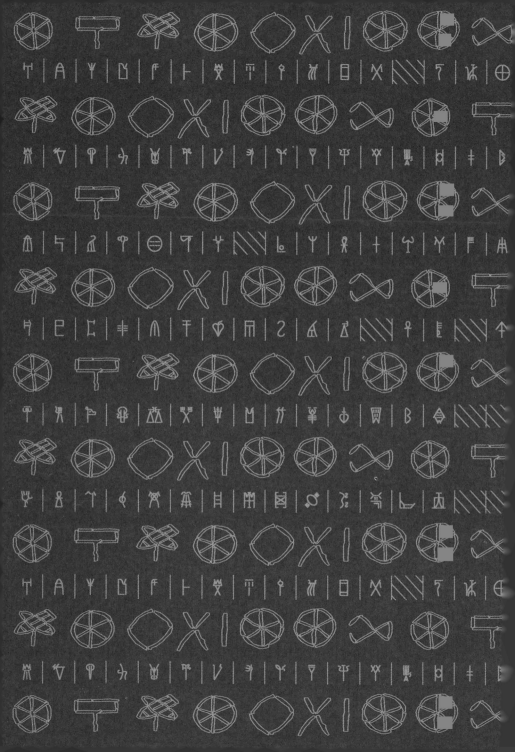

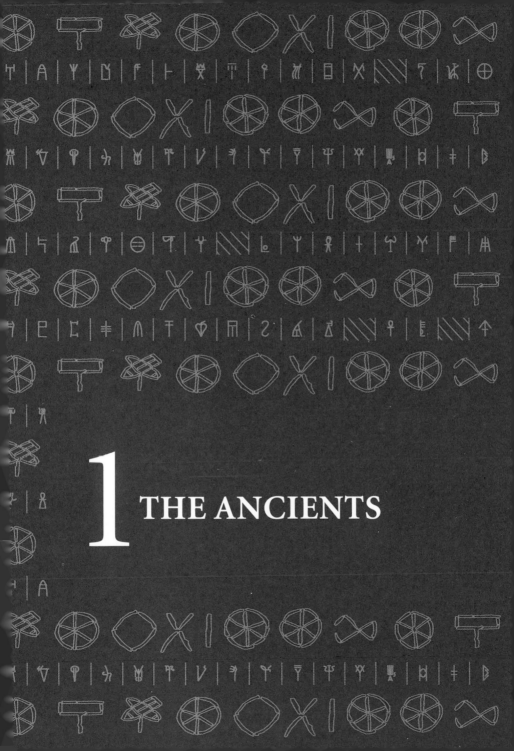

1 THE ANCIENTS

SUBSTITUTION AND TRANSPOSITION CIPHERS

Some of the languages used in the ancient world have long been lost, effectively rendering messages written in the characters of those languages into ciphers. The scripts of the Indus Valley civilization, which stretched from Afghanistan to India, were used for two millennia and involved pictograms of animals and everyday objects. Yet the language they represent remains a subject of controversy. The same problem faced the archaeologists who uncovered the linear scripts of ancient Crete.

Beyond the secrecy of unknown languages, early techniques for hiding messages were largely physical ones. In ancient China, for example, messages were written on silk, placed in balls of wax, and then swallowed by courier.

The cryptographic methods devised by the ancients were used largely during warfare and soon led to a war on a new front – not a physical one but one of the mind. They kick-started a war between cryptologist and cryptanalyst, codewriting against codebreaking. It is a war that continues to rage today.

The Early Coders

The ancient Greeks were among the first to use substitution ciphers in which letters in messages were substituted for other letters or symbols, while Roman emperor Julius Caesar is one of the best-known historical figures to have used substitution ciphers in communication. A simple shift of the alphabet was sufficient to hide messages sent to his supporters.

A cryptographic method that relies on changing the order of letters in a message rather than replacing them with other letters is known as a transposition cipher. The generals of Sparta used transposition to hide their military messages. Many of the ciphers in this chapter are substitution ciphers; however, in a transposition cipher, instead of replacing each letter of the plaintext alphabet, the letters are scrambled.

A simple example of a transposition cipher would be an anagram. However, in order to use a transposition cipher to send messages, the scrambling must be carried out according to some prearranged system. Consider the messages 'no attack on Monday' and 'attack noon Monday.' They are anagrams of the same letters and yet mean very different things.

One of the greatest advantages of a transposition cipher over a substitution cipher is its imperviousness to the use of frequency analysis (see pages 30–35). Frequency analysis on a transposition cipher can only tell us that the most common letter in a ciphertext is 'v', say, leading us to presume that it has replaced the letter 'e'; it tells us nothing about the position of letters in a deciphered code.

The Scytale

One of the earliest recorded uses of a transposition cipher is a rod-shaped object called a scytale, which was used by Spartan generals in ancient Greece. It involves two pieces of rounded wood, exactly alike in length and thickness. The sender keeps one and gives the other to his or her intended correspondent. When sending a message, the sender wraps a long strip of parchment tightly around the wood and writes the message on it, along the length of the rod. When unwrapped, the parchment simply shows a series of unrelated letters. The recipient wraps the parchment around his or her identical piece of wood to read off the intended message.

An illustrated reconstruction of a scytale. Used by the Spartans in Roman times, the message was only revealed by reading horizontally along a wooden rod of very specific measurements.

Using the cipher

Columnar transposition involves writing the plaintext message out in a grid whose columns are subsequently transposed. The number of columns depends on the length of a chosen key word and their transposition depends on the alphabetical order of those letters.

Let's say that the sender chooses the key **liberty**. He writes this at the top of a grid. Beneath each letter, he numbers them according to their position in the alphabet. The letter b is the earliest in the alphabet so this will become column 1; e is the next letter in the alphabet so this will be column 2 and so on. He then writes his message out underneath. If there are blank spaces at the end, he fills these with dummy letters.

L	I	B	E	R	T	Y
4	3	1	2	5	6	7
I	w	i	l	l	m	e
e	t	y	o	u	a	t
t	h	e	c	o	r	n
e	r	a	t	t	w	e
I	v	e	w	x	y	q

This grid shows the plaintext message 'I will meet you at the corner at twelve,' with four dummy characters. The extra characters are easy to discard once the meaning of the actual message has been revealed.

The columns of the plaintext are then shuffled into numerical order as below. The ciphertext is read down each column in turn to give the following message: IYEAELOCTWWTHRVIETELLUOTXMARWYETNEQ. The recipient is given the keyword separately and uses this to recreate the original grid.

B	E	I	L	R	T	Y
1	2	3	4	5	6	7
i	l	w	l	l	m	e
y	o	t	e	u	a	t
e	c	h	t	o	r	n
a	t	r	e	t	w	e
e	w	v	l	x	y	q

The rail-fence, or zigzag, cipher uses an imaginary fence with the successive letters of a plaintext message written zigzagging across each rail of the fence as shown above.

The ciphertext is then obtained by reading across each rail and running these together to yield: **GHDIBOOQNDLVRATAEEG**. The recipient only needs to know the number of rails in order to decrypt the message.

g				h				d				i				b		
	o		o		q		n		d		l		v		r		a	
		t				a				e				e				g

INDUS SCRIPT

A 4,000-year-old series of inscriptions from Asia has so far resisted attempts to reveal its meaning, yet there are tantalizing signs that the script can be cracked.

The Indus Valley civilization existed in a large region that covered parts of Afghanistan, Pakistan, and India between 3300 and 1300 BCE, with its population numbering as many as five million. Whether this Bronze Age civilization was literate or not remains a point of controversy for historians and archaeologists, and much of the debate centres on what is known as the Indus script.

Most Indus script is found on stone seals. In 1875 Sir Alexander Cunningham, the archaeological surveyor

An authentic and typical Bronze Age seal featuring a unicorn. The meaning of the Indus script on the top right still escapes modern codebreakers.

to the government of India, published the first drawings of stone seals found in Harappa, Pakistan. Since then, thousands of seals, tablets, and engraved pots have been discovered, each bearing a number of simple symbols and pictures.

Understanding the cipher

The inscriptions that have been discovered so far contain a corpus of more than 400 different basic symbols, with around 2,000 different variations. This number has led scholars to the conclusion that Indus script contains

Indus symbols discovered near Dholavira, western India. The sheer abundance of symbols has pushed scholars to the conclusion that they represent words and ideas, rather than letters.

characters representing both words and symbols. They dismiss the idea that the characters represent individual letters, simply because there are so many of them when compared to, for example, the Latin alphabet. Conversely, the idea that the characters *only* represent words or ideas is also ruled out, because there are so few compared to, say, the more than 100,000 pictograms and ideograms used in non-simplified Chinese. All of the inscriptions are short, with most just a few symbols long, and this has led scholars to believe that many of the scripts are names, job titles or familial connections. Some scholars have suggested that Indus script represents an early form of Sanskrit or a Dravidian language common to the region, such as Tamil or Kannada, although no conclusive proof has been established.

One starting point for deciphering unknown scripts is to use the rebus principle – the idea that symbols can be used to represent homophones (words that sound the same but have different meanings, such as bear and bare in English). One such symbol in Indus script is that of the fish. In many Dravidian languages, the word for fish is *meen*, which also has the homophone 'star'. The fish symbol is often followed by a number symbol and some have deduced that these combinations refer to asterisms – groups of prominent stars – such as the Pleiades (fish and the number six). The reasoning for this is that in Old Tamil, the name for the Pleiades is *aru-meen*, or six stars.

CODEBREAKERS OF HISTORY

KOBER, VENTRIS AND CHADWICK

Clay tablets inscribed with secret languages were found in the Palace of Knossos on the island of Crete at the turn of the twentieth century. One took fifty years to crack; the other remains a mystery to this day.

The Palace of Knossos was one of the greatest archaeological discoveries of the twentieth century. Besides the complex of buildings, beneath which the legendary Minotaur is said to have dwelt, the site also yielded other secrets. The man who unearthed the palace, British archaeologist Arthur Evans, found thousands of clay tablets bearing two types of linear script, subsequently named Linear A and B. (Linear, in this sense, means made up of lines as opposed to more pictorial hieroglyphic inscriptions.)

The finds at Knossos, coupled with other discoveries made elsewhere, indicate that Linear A was prevalent throughout central and eastern Crete, and possibly the wider Aegean region, by the end of the Middle Minoan period and during the early part of the Late Minoan period.

By the end of the fifteenth century BCE, and the early part of the fourteenth, Linear A disappeared and Linear B inscriptions become more prevalent. However, Linear B is not simply a later outgrowth of Linear A. Arthur Evans's belief was that the majority of Linear B inscriptions were business records, such as accounts or inventories.

Linear B has approximately 200 different symbols: 87 phonetic signs and more than 100 ideographic symbols representing things such as chariot wheels, weapons, cereals, and domesticated animals.

Alice Kober, assistant professor of classics at Brooklyn College, City University of New York, broke the back of Linear B by analyzing frequency of appearance and creating a database of more than 180,000 index cards. She concluded that whatever language was represented was an inflected language – that is, a language in which a word changes according to number, gender, and case.

Kober died in 1950 and did not live to see Michael Ventris and John Chadwick crack the secrets of Linear B three years later. After studying the patterns of symbols, the pair concluded that, contrary to the view of Evans, the language represented by Linear B was actually Mycenaean Greek. They reached this conclusion from looking at the frequency of word endings and making educated guesses on which symbols referred to which syllables. From an initial guess for the syllables representing words ending in -u, Ventris and Chadwick then made other associations with Greek syllables to see whether inscriptions would yield recognizable words.

Using their proposed identification of the symbols of Linear B, the inscriptions eventually yielded a number of place-names relating to Crete and Knossos, and other words that were clearly identifiable as Greek in origin. This discovery was a major one. Not only did it indicate that Greek was a written language several hundred years earlier than previously thought, but also that there was a Greek-speaking culture on Crete at the time the scripts were written, suggesting it was under the control of the mainland.

Although Linear A and B share a number of symbols, placing the Ventris and Chadwick syllabic substitutions into Linear A inscriptions produces no intelligible words. So far, it is not possible to ascertain whether Linear A appears to relate a known language.

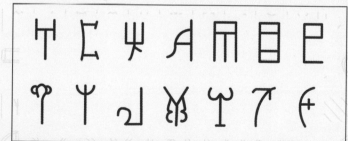

A selection of Linear A symbols. Discovered along with the Palace of Knossos in Crete, the solution is still uncracked today.

PHAISTOS DISC

A clay disc found a century ago may contain the
first example of movable-type printing, yet what the
inscriptions actually mean has been intensely debated.

On 3 July 1908, Italian archaeologist Luigi Pernier, from Florence, was on
a dig in the basements of buildings close to the Minoan palace of Phaistos
in southern Crete. During the excavations, Pernier unearthed a small, clay
disc measuring around 15 centimetres (6 inches) in diameter, marked on
both sides with spirals of unknown characters.

The setting in which the disc was found led Pernier to believe that it
dated from the Middle Minoan period, around 1850 to 1600 BCE, although
others argue that it could be from a few centuries later. Of particular
interest is the manner in which the symbols have been placed on the disc:
using premade stamps of the symbols rather than by carving. The stamps
would have been impressed on the soft clay and the disc then hardened by
firing. The method – not seen elsewhere in this era – leads some to suggest
that it is the first example of movable-type printing.

Understanding the cipher

The disc contains 242 symbols in total, of which 45 are unique. The
symbols are pictograms representing a range of subjects, including women,
children, weapons, birds and plants. They are remarkably distinct and
detailed. The symbols are divided into groups, separated by vertical lines,
assumed by some to be word breaks. There are also carved diagonal strokes
that may indicate the end of a paragraph.

Most scholars believe that each side of the disc was stamped from the
outside edge toward the centre, since some of the central characters appear
somewhat cramped.

Several claim to have deciphered the Phaistos Disc, but the brevity
of the script, and the fact that there are no other texts that use the same
symbols, means that there is unlikely ever to be consensus on its true

The Phaistos Disc, currently on display at the Heraklion Archaeological Museum, Crete, has sparked debate among scholars; one suggestion is that it is a calendar.

meaning. Several scholars, both professional and amateur, have suggested that the disc is an astronomical calendar. In 1980, Andis Kaulins made a statistical analysis of the symbols and compared their frequency and distribution to texts in ancient Greek as well as Latvian and Lithuanian. Using a grid of syllabic values, he then argued that the text is actually a mathematical proof of two geometric postulates that are later attributed to Euclid.

Scholars have put forward a wide range of possible linguistic origins for the symbols on the disc, including Old Estonian, Tatarish-Turkish and even Indian. Others believe that the language is more localized in origin, probably from Greece and, most likely of all, from Crete itself. However, others still dispute the Cretan origin, suggesting that the clay does not resemble others found on the island and that the symbols show a lack of similarity with known Cretan hieroglyphs.

Pre-Columbian scholar Dr Michael Coe has suggested that a thermoluminescence dating test be carried out to determine its exact age. Until then, theories about the disc's meaning will continue to proliferate.

ATBASH CIPHER

Atbash is a monoalphabetic substitution cipher proposed by Hebrew scholars to explain the appearance of unusual place-names in the Bible.

In the Book of Jeremiah, 25:26, there is a passage that reads:

> 'And all the kings of the north, near and far, one after the other – all the kingdoms on the face of the Earth. And after all of them, the king of Sheshach will drink it too.'

The passage relates to the prophet Jeremiah being sent to various nations to force their kings to drink from the Cup of God's Wrath, predicting disaster. The kings, peoples and places referenced in the passages before this – Moab, the Philistines, Tyre, Sidon and more – have long been known among biblical scholars, yet Sheshach remains a mystery and may not be a real place.

Some believe that the Hebrew scholars writing in the sixth century BCE used something called the Atbash cipher to hide the original name of the city – Babel, or Babylon. Elsewhere in Jeremiah (51:1), there is a reference to another place called Leb Kamai. Again, scholars believe this to be a coded mention of Babylon. But is this a real cipher or just wishful thinking? Some experts have pointed to the fact that Babylon is mentioned elsewhere in Jeremiah, which means that there appears to be no compelling reason to resort to concealment here.

A Medieval depiction of King Nimrod of Babylon and the Tower of Babel. It is debated whether Hebrew scholars used ciphers to conceal the name of this city and its famous tower as some named places cannot be traced.

Even so, Atbash is an interesting system for cryptologists to learn. Anyone who knows that an Atbash cipher has been used simply uses the encryption process in reverse to decipher the message. Without knowledge of the encryption system, codebreakers need to turn to frequency analysis for individual letters (see pages 30–35) and, for a longer piece, to analysis of frequently occurring digraphs and trigraphs (see pages 50–53).

Using the cipher

Atbash is a simple, monoalphabetic substitution cipher. The method of encryption is to replace the first letter of the alphabet with the last, the second letter with the second last and so on. In Hebrew, this would be replacing *aleph* with *tav*, *beth* with *shin* and so on. The cipher takes its name from the initial sounds of these letters A-T-B-SH.

The Atbash cipher can be used in any language. With the Latin alphabet, the corresponding table would be as follows:

Plaintext	a	b	c	d	e	f	g	h	i	j	k	l	m	n	o	p	q	r	s	t	u	v	w	x	y	z
Ciphertext	Z	Y	X	W	V	U	T	S	R	Q	P	O	N	M	L	K	J	I	H	G	F	E	D	C	B	A

Often the table is truncated as follows, where a plaintext letter is replaced by the ciphertext letter above or below.

a	b	c	d	e	f	g	h	i	j	k	l	m
z	y	x	w	v	u	t	s	r	q	p	o	n

POLYBIUS SQUARE

We know much about the ancient Greeks through the historian Polybius. It is also from his chronicles of Grecian life that we learn of an ancient cipher method.

Much of what we know about the rise of Rome as a world power during the second century BCE can be attributed to the Greek historian Polybius and his history of the Greek world, called simply *The Histories*.

In Book X of *The Histories*, Polybius describes a method of encrypting telegraphic signals that has since become known as the Polybius square, although Polybius himself admits that he did not invent it.

Using the cipher

The method involves dividing the alphabet into five groups of letters. The Greek alphabet has 24 letters, so we divide it into four groups of five and one of four, each written on a separate, numbered tablet.

	1	2	3	4	5
1	A	B	Γ	Δ	E
2	Z	H	Θ	I	K
3	Λ	M	N	Ξ	O
4	Π	Π	Σ	T	Ψ
5	Φ	Ξ	Ψ	Ω	

Two people who wish to communicate at a distance need to equip themselves with: the numbered tablets, a telescope with two tubes (although Polybius did not have this luxury), ten lit torches and a pair of screens. Then, according to Polybius:

'The man who is going to signal is in the first place to raise two torches and wait until the other replies by doing the same. This is for the purpose of conveying to each other that they are both at attention. These torches having been lowered, the dispatcher of the message will now raise the first set of torches on the left side indicating which tablet is to be consulted – that is, one torch if it is the first, two if it is the second, and so on. Next he will raise the second set on the right on the same principle to indicate what letter of the tablet the receiver should write down.'

The system is prone to error through misidentification of the number of torches (the screens are used to hide those not in use). One missed signal throws the whole system. The system is also time-consuming:

	1	2	3	4	5
1	a	b	c	d	e
2	f	g	h	i/j	k
3	l	m	n	o	p
4	q	r	s	y	u
5	v	w	x	y	z

Polybius suggests abbreviating messages as much as possible. For easier use, the separate tablets are often condensed into a single encryption table known as a Polybius square. The table above shows how the system could be used to encrypt messages using a Latin alphabet. (Note that when used with Latin alphabets, 'i' and 'j' are generally used interchangeably.) Say we want to encrypt the following plaintext message: 'enemies at the gate'. You take each letter of the plaintext and find it in the square. Write down the row number and then the column number. You could signal this using a system of torches, or by writing it as a sequence of numbers as a ciphertext as follows: **15331 53224154311444423152211445**. The recipient would then use the same table to reconstruct the plaintext, taking pairs of numbers in turn.

CAESAR SHIFT CIPHER

This simple cipher involves shifting the alphabet by one or more letters and is attributed to Roman emperor Julius Caesar.

The Caesar shift cipher is one of the simplest substitution ciphers – that is, one in which the letters of a plaintext message are replaced by the corresponding letters in a ciphertext alphabet.

While the Caesar shift cipher was almost certainly not invented by Julius Caesar, it is most closely associated with him because of the following reference in Suetonius's *Lives of the Twelve Caesars*:

'There are also letters of [Caesar's] to Cicero, as well as to his intimates on private affairs, and in the latter, if he had anything confidential to say, he wrote it in cipher, that is, by so changing the order of the letters of the alphabet, that not a word could be made out. If anyone wishes to decipher these, and get at their meaning, he must substitute the fourth letter of the alphabet, namely D, for A, and so with the others.'

A hand-drawn replica of an antique bust of Roman Emperor Julius Caesar, after whom the Caesar shift cipher was named.

How easy it is to break the Caesar shift cipher depends on what information you have. If you know that a Caesar shift has been used, you can use a brute-force attack to crack the ciphertext. All you have to do is try all possible ROTN transformations (see below) until you find the correct one. If you don't know that a Caesar shift cipher has been used, you can employ frequency analysis (see pages 30–35).

Using the cipher

The simplest way to use the Caesar shift cipher is by writing out two alphabets – a plaintext one and a ciphertext one with the letters shifted by a given number of places. The one suggested in the Suetonius biography would look like this:

Plaintext	a	b	c	d	e	f	g	h	i	j	k	l	m	n	o	p	q	r	s	t	u	v	w	x	y	z
Ciphertext	D	E	F	G	H	I	J	K	L	M	N	O	P	Q	R	S	T	U	V	W	X	Y	Z	A	B	C

Encrypting a message is a simple matter of replacing the letter in the top row with the corresponding letter in the bottom row. For example, 'beware the Ides of March' becomes EHZDUH WKH LGHV RI PDUFK.

Caesar's correspondents would just need to know the number of places by which the alphabet had been shifted in order to reveal the original message. This type of transformation is known as ROTN where N is the number of places by which the alphabet has been shifted. Caesar's three-place shift is therefore a ROT3 transformation.

To the modern eye, the cipher seems easy and it is indeed the first cipher that many children encounter. In the first century BCE, however, Caesar's messages must have seemed gibberish. The Emperor's inner thoughts, whether shared with Cicero or even Cleopatra, were safe.

ᚠᚢᚦᚨᚱᚲᚷᚹᚺᚾᛁᛇ

ᛈᛚᛅᛞᛜᛗᛝᛖᚽᛏᛊᛘᛁᛣᛟ

ᛏᛜᚿᛢᛝᛒᛥᛤᛁᚤᛦᛧᛁᛏᛤⴲ

ᚠᚢᚦᚨᚱᚲᚷᚹᚺᚾᛁᛇ

ᛈᛚᛅᛞᛜᛗᛝᛖᚽᛏᛊᛘᛁᛣᛟ

ᛏᛜᚿᛢᛝᛒᛥᛤᛁᚤᛦᛧᛁᛏᛤⴲ

2 THE SONS
OF WISDOM

NEW LIGHT IN THE DARK AGES

As historians learn more about the period between the fall of the Roman Empire and the Renaissance – despite the paucity of written records from this era – they tend to use the somewhat derogatory term 'Dark Ages' less frequently. Developments in writing and codebreaking continued during this time, perhaps because of, rather than in spite of, the conflicts that were occurring, particularly in Europe.

In Ireland, locals may have resorted to the use of a secret alphabet known as ogham to hide messages from invaders. Ogham, which appears on stone monuments around Ireland and parts of Britain, bears similarities to runic ciphers used by the Vikings as they fought their way across Europe. Elsewhere, the techniques of code-writing remained very much the same – hiding messages through steganographic methods and using simple monoalphabetic substitutions such as the Caesar shift cipher (see page 26).

Frequency Analysis

Many early ciphers such as the Caesar shift seem simple and trivial today, yet without knowing the encryption method used, codebreakers in the first few centuries of the Christian Era were stymied.

In fact, it would be another 900 years after Julius Caesar's time before someone worked out a way to crack such simple substitution ciphers. That credit goes to the Iraqi philosopher and mathematician Abu Yusuf Yaqub Ibn Ishaq al-Kindi, born in Basra in 801 CE.

In his manuscript *On Deciphering Cryptographic Messages*, al-Kindi outlines a scheme based on using the relative frequency of letters

A complete set of English language Scrabble tiles, where the frequency of letters in the language reflects how often the letters appear.

within a language to help crack messages. He said the system would be reasonably clear to the sons of wisdom, and out of reach of the uninformed and laymen. This system, known as frequency analysis, is perhaps the most powerful codebreaking technique ever conceived.

The basis of frequency analysis can be understood by looking at the letter tiles in the board game Scrabble. The image opposite shows a set of tiles with the number of points each letter scores in the corner. It is immediately evident that there are more 'e's than any other letter and that they only score one point; there is just one 'z' and it scores ten points. The reason behind the scoring system in Scrabble is that 'e' is the most commonly used letter in the English language and 'z' is the least frequently used.

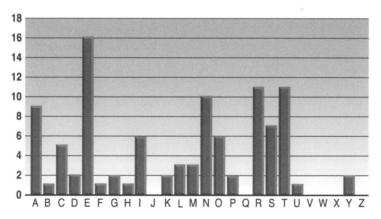

Cornell English letter frequency chart.

A study by Cornell University of 40,000 English words found the frequency of letters illustrated above. It demonstrates that 'e' is by far the most common letter in English. So how does this help a codebreaker? Imagine we have the following ciphertext that we wish to crack:

DOO KXPDQ EHLQJV DUH ERUQ IUHH DQG HTXDO LQ GLJQLWB DQG ULJKWV. WKHB DUH HQGRZHG ZLWK UHDVRQ DQG FRQVFLHQFH DQG VKRXOG DFW WRZDUGV RQH DQRWKHU LQ D VSLULW RI EURWKHUKRRG. HYHUBRQH LV HQWLWOHG WR DOO WKH ULJKWV DQG IUHHGRPV VHW IRUWK LQ WKLV GHFODUDWLRQ, ZLWKRXW GLVWLQFWLRQ RI D NLQG, VXFK DV UDFH, FRORXU, VHD, ODQJXDJH, UHOLJLRQ, SROLWLFDO RU RWKHU RSLQLRQ, QDWLRQDO RU VRFLDO RULJLQ, SURSHUWB, ELUWK RU RWKHU VWDWXV. IXUWKHUPRUH, QR GLVWLQFWLRQ VKDOO EH PDGH RQ WKH EDVLV RI WKH SROLWLFDO, MXULVGLFWLRQDO RU LQWHUQDWLRQDO VWDWXV RI WKH FRXQWUB RU WHUULWRUB WR ZKLFK D SHUVRQ EHORQJV, ZKHWKHU LW EH LQGHSHQGHQW, WUXVW, QRQ-VHOI-JRYHUQLQJ RU XQGHU DQB RWKHU OLPLWDWLRQ RI VRYHUHLJQWB. HYHUBRQH KDV WKH ULJKW WR OLIH, OLEHUWB DQG WKH VHFXULWB RI SHUVRQ. QR RQH VKDOO EH KHOG LQ VODYHUB RU VHUYLWXGH; VODYHUB DQG WKH VODYH WUDGH VKDOO EH SURKLELWHG LQ DOO WKHLU IRUPV. QR RQH VKDOO EH VXEMHFWHG WR WRUWXUH RU WR FUXHO, LQKXPDQ RU GHJUDGLQJ WUHDWPHQW RU SXQLVKPHQW. HYHUBRQH KDV WKH ULJKW WR UHFRJQLWLRQ HYHUBZKHUH DV D SHUVRQ EHIRUH WKH ODZ. DOO DUH HTXDO EHIRUH WKH ODZ DQG DUH HQWLWOHG ZLWKRXW DQB GLVFULPLQDWLRQ WR HTXDO SURWHFWLRQ RI WKH ODZ.

The approach is to count how often each character appears and plot it in a similar chart to the one opposite. Given its overwhelming frequency, it is safe to assume that the ciphertext character H represents the plaintext character 'e'. Indeed that is the case.

If it is known that the cipher is a Caesar shift cipher, then working out the rest of the message is trivial. If 'e' is encrypted as H, this is a ROT3 transformation and we can use the same two alphabets that we used on page 27 to encrypt the phrase 'beware the ides of March'. Doing so reveals that our plaintext starts with the sentence: 'All human beings are born free and equal in dignity and rights'. The ciphertext is the beginning of the United Nations' Universal Declaration of Human Rights.

Frequency analysis is a powerful decryption tool against other forms of cipher. With a Caesar shift, the discovery of the letter E reveals the entire

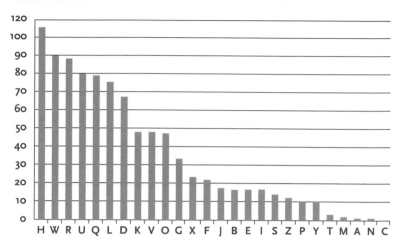

When analyzed, the cipher text above shows a clear preference for certain characters. The codebreaker can then make an educated guess concerning which ciphers and Latin letters are corresponding.

scheme. However, if a more complicated substitution than a rotation of the alphabet is used, frequency analysis can discover those other letters, too.

Looking again at the frequency chart above, the next most common letters are **v, D, K, W, L, Q, O, R, U,** and **G**. In the Cornell analysis, the next most common English letters are 't, a, o, i, n, s, r, h, d and l'. Although the correspondences are not exact, it is simply a matter of trial and error in placing these plaintext letters within the ciphertext to see whether common words are revealed.

Remember each language has its own distribution of frequencies so you need to know the original language of the encoded ciphertext. You can see this at work in Scrabble too – versions of the game in different languages have quite different distributions of letters and points.

OGHAM ALPHABET

This mystical alphabet is found on stone monuments around the Irish Sea and dates back to at least the fourth century.

Dotted around Ireland, Wales, Scotland and parts of England are around 400 stone monuments bearing a series of carved marks at their edges. Most of the marked stones date from the fifth and sixth centuries, but some are from much earlier. On a number of the monuments, the marks appear to be random gougings, while on others they clearly represent something now recognized as an alphabet called ogham (pronounced AHG-m or OH-ehm).

The origins of ogham are not clear. Some scholars believe it was invented by Irish speakers as a cipher to hide messages from invaders from Roman Britain who used the Latin alphabet. Others suggest that early Christians in Ireland invented the language as a way of writing down Primitive Irish. Most of what we know about ogham comes from a fourteenth-century manuscript known as the *Book of Ballymote*, a re-scribed collection of earlier writings. One of the works included in the *Book of Ballymote* is known as *Auraicept na n-Éces*, dating from around the seventh century CE, which includes details of several different versions of ogham. It says:

> *'These are their signs: right of stem, left of stem, athwart of stem, through stem, about stem. Thus is a tree climbed, to wit, treading on the root of the tree first with thy right hand first and thy left hand after. Then with the stem, and against it, and through it and about it.'*

The *Book of Ballymote* proved to be the key that was needed to crack the ogham mystery, explaining the correspondence between the feda (ogham letters) and letters in the Latin alphabet. Many of the inscriptions are names or descriptions of people, suggesting that the stones are gravestones or property boundary markers.

Using the cipher

The ogham alphabet has twenty letters or *feda*, divided into four groups or aicmí (meaning family.) Each *aicme* contains five letters. There are also five additional symbols, called *forfeda*, used for diphthongs, such as 'ea' and 'ae'.

The letters are represented by strokes relative to a vertical line or stem. On the stone monuments, the stem itself is not explicitly carved, but is usually a corner or edge of the stone. It is useful to note that ogham on stone inscriptions is intended to be read from the right-hand side, bottom up, over the top and down the left-hand side. When written in manuscript, it is read from right to left. This cipher is sometimes called the Celtic Tree language, as most of the letters are named after trees. For example, **b** or *bithe* means birch, while **c** or *coll* means hazel.

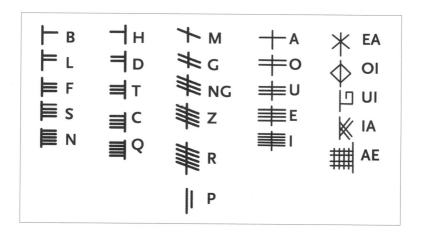

The complete ogham alphabet with the corresponding Latin letters. The letters, called feda, *are divided into* aicmí *(families). The symbols used for diphthongs are called* forfeda.

CODEBREAKERS OF HISTORY

JONAS NORDBY

For much of the first millennium, the Germanic peoples of northern Europe used a system known as runes for their alphabets, as opposed to the Latin alphabet that dominates today. Runic letters are angular and spindly compared to their Latin counterparts. From around the fifth to the eleventh century, a system known as the *futhorc* was in use in Scandinavia. The Vikings were very fond of using ciphers to hide their messages and used a variety of symbols to replace the runic letters, including tents, trees with branches, and even beards.

In 1955, one of the most important archaeological discoveries linked to the understanding of runes was made in the Norwegian city of Bergen when more than six hundred wooden sticks inscribed with runes were unearthed. This trove revealed that runes were not just used in limited circumstances but had been a widespread system of writing. The sticks revealed names and business correspondence as well as personal messages – sometimes rude ones. Some of the sticks were inscribed with a hitherto unknown method of cipher, which was subsequently named the Jötunvillur code or the Norse code.

Many of the rune ciphers use different symbols, but employ the same basic method of hiding information. They divide the runic alphabet into three groups of letters or *ætts*. The image opposite shows one cipher that uses trees and branches. The branches and roots on the left indicate which *ætt* is being

A sample of the Anglo-Saxon runes, collectively known as futhorc. *The runes were the dominant script in northern Europe for much of the first millennium.*

A selection of the symbols that were used in the Jötunvillur code. Six hundred sticks with these inscriptions were unearthed in Bergen, Norway in 1955.

used while those on the right indicate which letter within the *ætt* is being referred to.

The Jötunvillur code was broken in early 2014 by runologist K. Jonas Nordby while studying for his doctorate in cryptic runes at the University of Oslo, Norway. He did this by focusing on one particular rune stick found in the Bergen hoard, in which the same two names were written in both runes and the mysterious code. In much the same way as scholars before him used the famous Rosetta Stone to decode Egyptian hieroglyphics, Nordby used the runes on the stick to decode the Jötunvillur code. He knew that both the ciphers showed the names Sigurd and Lavrans. His breakthrough was to realize that, in the Jötunvillur code, each rune is replaced by the rune that represents the last letter of its full runic name. So the rune for **b**, *bjarkan*, is replaced with the rune for 'n'.

The correspondences are shown below. Note that several runes in the code are enciphered as the same rune, which made it especially hard to crack.

Plaintext	f	u	þ	o	r	k	h	n	i	a	s	t	b	m	l	y
Runic character name	fé	úr	purs	óss	reið	kaun	hagal	nauð	íss	ár	sól	týr	bjarkan	maðr	logr	ýr
Jötunvillur	e	r	s	s	þ	n	l	þ	s	r	l	r	n	r	r	r

Runologist K. Jonas Nordby broke the Jötunvillur code in 2014 using this cipher alphabet. He focused on just one stick from the Bergen hoard.

RONGORONGO

The stone faces or *mo'ai* carvings of Easter Island are not the only mystery concerning this remote place. A small number of tablets exist bearing stylized symbols of plants and animals but no one can decipher what they mean.

The island, 2000 miles from the next inhabited island in the Pacific, also lacks vegetation. It was not always this way, however. Easter Island's native trees have all been felled, leaving it a bleak and desolate place. Perhaps some of these mysteries could be explained if only we were able to decipher thousands of highly stylized symbols of birds, turtles, people and plants on a series of wooden tablets that date from the height of Easter Island's civilization between the thirteenth and seventeenth centuries.

In 1864, Father Eugène Eyraud visited Easter Island in order to convert its inhabitants to Catholicism and found 'wooden tablets or sticks covered in several sorts of hieroglyphic characters'. Four years later, Florentin-Étienne 'Tepano' Jaussen, the Bishop of Tahiti, received a gift from the converted islanders – a haft of hair wrapped around one of these tablets.

The iconic mo'ai *statues on Easter Island, where wooden tablets bearing undeciphered code dating between the thirteenth and seventeenth centuries have been found.*

The bishop, recognizing its potential importance, asked Easter Island's new priest Father Hippolyte Roussel (Eyraud had died of tuberculosis by this time) to see if he could gather more tablets and find someone able to translate them. In Tahiti, Jaussen found a laborer, Metoro Tau'a Ure, who was able to explain some of the tablets and, together, they spent the next few years recording data. However, this work did not lead to the code being deciphered. This code has since become known as rongorongo, which means 'to chant or recite' in the native Rapa Nui language.

The biggest step toward an understanding of rongorongo was the publication in 1958 of a full catalog of the glyphs, *Grundlagen zur Entzifferung der Osterinselschrift* by German ethnologist Thomas Barthel.

Barthel's first step in understanding rongorongo was his recognition that because there were more than 120 different symbols which were combined in thousands of different ways, they were more likely to represent words or concepts than letters. He tracked down the journal of Tepano Jaussen and used it to help him identify some of the tablets as prayers. He also became the first to show what some of the script meant – he correctly identified a section of one wooden tablet as a lunar calendar.

In 1995, linguist Steven Fischer claimed to have decoded one of the most interesting elements in the rongorongo corpus, the Santiago staff – a 150-centimetre (five foot) long wooden pole bearing hundreds of glyphs. Fischer proposed that the staff was covered with creation chants of the form 'A copulated with B and begat C'. Others have since disputed Fischer's claim as it appears to lead to nonsensical interpretations of the other tablets.

Using the cipher

What we know today of rongorongo comes from the 26 wooden tablets that remain. (There are even doubts about the authenticity of a small number of these.) There were not always so few – when Father Eyraud first visited there were tablets in most huts. The inhabitants had forgotten the meaning of the symbols and deforestation of the island meant that many of the tablets were burned; others were used as fishing line holders and lost.

The iconic mo'ai *statues on Easter Island, where wooden tablets bearing undeciphered code dating between the thirteenth and seventeenth centuries have been found.*

The rongorongo symbols are believed to relate to Rapanui, the Polynesian language spoken only by the inhabitants of Easter Island. The 26 tablets that remain feature hundreds of different animal, plant and human glyphs that have been carved into the wood using obsidian, shark's teeth or other natural objects. In total, the tablets contain about 15,000 glyphs that are legible.

   Rongorongo is written using a system called reverse boustrophedon. The reader begins at bottom right and reads towards the left. At the end of the line, the reader then rotates the text by 180 degrees and reads the next line, continuing all the way to the top. The letters are believed to have been carved onto the tablets using obsidian flakes or shark's teeth.

VOYNICH MANUSCRIPT

A bizarre-looking book written some time during the Middle Ages was rediscovered a century ago. Not only does the language in the book remain unknown, but the tome also contains some unusual diagrams.

In 1912, the Jesuit college at Villa Mondragone in Frascati, Italy, was in urgent need of funds and decided to sell some of its manuscripts. Polish-born London antiquarian bookseller Wilfrid Voynich bought thirty of them, among them something most unusual. He believed that the manuscript in question dated from the late thirteenth century because of the vellum material, the calligraphy and pigments used. He settled on the Franciscan friar Roger Bacon as the probable author. William Newbold, who worked on a credible attempt to decipher the manuscript, also believed Roger Bacon to be the author. However, in 2009, the University of Arizona carbon-dated samples of the vellum and placed it between 1404 and 1438, possibly ruling out Bacon as author.

Understanding the cipher

The codex, amounting to 240 pages at the time of Voynich's acquisition, but with some pages clearly missing, is written in an unknown script, comprising some 170,000 symbols or glyphs. Of those 170,000, there appears to be an alphabet of between 20 and 30 characters used with regular frequency. On virtually every page, there is also an illustration. Many of these show botanical specimens, others show zodiacal constellations and astronomical drawings, while the more unusual ones show 'miniature female nudes, most with swelled abdomens'. Many of the botanical specimens have not been clearly identified, although American botanist Hugh O'Neill suggested that one showed a sunflower and another the capsicum – if the origin of the manuscript is European then this would date it to after 1493 when Columbus returned with these species.

There is a consensus that the language used in the manuscript is European and probably Medieval Latin or Medieval English. Newbold believed the language was Latin and that each pair of letters in the manuscript represented a single letter in the plaintext alphabet. Before his death, he had managed to decipher a few pages using this method and used his findings to claim that Bacon had invented the telescope long before its actual invention.

Some scholars suggest that the meaning is actually hidden using something known as a grille cipher (see page 56), while others who have failed to decode the manuscript believe that it is merely a hoax.

Using the cipher

In 2014, Stephen Bax, Professor of Applied Linguistics at the University of Bedfordshire, took a new approach to attempting to decode the manuscript. His method was to identify the botanical specimens and then attempt to link them with the names of those plants.

Bax suggested this 'bottom-up' approach, rather than using computers to crunch the information in the manuscript, because of the success of such techniques in decoding Egyptian hieroglyphics and Linear B. By analyzing other medieval herbal manuscripts, Bax postulated that the name of the illustrated plant was likely to be the first word or appear in the first line of the text on the same page.

His first attempt to use this technique focused on pages 15 and 16 of the manuscript. He noted the repeated occurrence of a text pattern, referred to as OROR. Bax suggested that this might represent the Arabic/Hebrew word *arar*, meaning juniper, and that the accompanying illustration depicted the *Juniperus oxycedrus*, common to the eastern Mediterranean area. He went on to propose identifications of nine further words and approximate sound values of 14 more symbols and clusters. At this stage, Bax suggests that the identification of these words indicates that the Voynich manuscript is not a hoax nor an elaborate cipher. His view is that it is an exploratory treatise setting out descriptions of the natural world and that it 'appears to act as a type of manual for interpreting and transmitting information across cultures'.

A page from the Voynich Manuscript, a curious book discovered in 1912 but which was probably written in the Middle Ages. It is now a part of Yale University's Beinecke Rare Book and Manuscript Library.

CISTERCIAN CIPHER

Medieval monks used this system as a quick way of recording numerical information, rather than as a way to conceal meaning.

Some ciphers are just a quicker way of writing. Indeed, shorthand systems such as Pitman, Teeline and Duployan can be considered as cipher systems. There are also shorthand cipher forms that can be used for writing numbers as well as words, one of which hails from the Middle Ages. In 2001, author David A. King published his work *The Ciphers of the Monks*. The book is an extensive treatment of the many cipher systems used in Europe at the time.

According to King, the Cistercian cipher was a more advanced version of a numerical cipher introduced to England by the monk John of Basingstoke in the early thirteenth century. This cipher was a simple method of writing the numbers 1 to 99.

The more advanced Cistercian was a cipher that was developed by monks of that order in the late thirteenth century on the Franco-Belgian border and then used for the next two centuries all over Europe. The cipher was used for numbering pages in manuscripts, creating indexes as well as lists. Evidence of its use comes from more than 20 surviving manuscripts originating in countries across Europe, from Sweden to Spain. The cipher has also been found on a medieval astrolabe from the Picardy region, a device for predicting the positions of the planets and for working out local time at a given latitude.

The astrolabe was presented as a gift from a certain Paschasius Berselius to one Hadrianus Amerotius in 1522 but it dates from an earlier period, probably the end of the thirteenth century. It was offered for sale at auction at Christie's in London in 1991 and it was this event that generated renewed interest in the cipher.

The cipher bridged a gap between the use of Roman numerals and the introduction of Hindu-Arabic numerals. It does not appear to have been used for calculation purposes and this may have led to its demise. Although the cipher itself fell out of use, the monastic ciphers were generally influential.

King says, 'The monastic ciphers in both their manifestations – numerical and alphabetical – were influential in the development of Renaissance shorthands and secret codes. From the sixteenth to the nineteenth century they were featured in various works on numerical notations. They were adopted by the Freemasons in Paris in 1780.'

Using the cipher

A number of different cipher systems were used by the monks, based on a series of horizontal or vertical marks, with added appendages to indicate units, tens, hundreds and thousands.

The system used on the Berselius astrolabe and in many manuscripts employs a vertical stem and nine appendages. Units are indicated to the top right of the stem, tens to the top left, hundreds to the bottom right and thousands to the bottom left. The system is shown in the image below, along with the method of combining these.

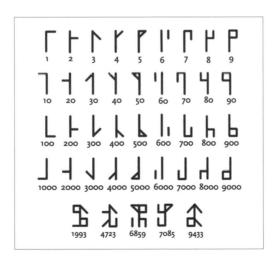

The Cistercian cipher which was used by monks across Europe to enumerate pages or lists.

CODEBREAKERS OF HISTORY

IBN AL-DURAYHIM

Sunni scholar Ibn al-Durayhim was born in 1312 in the city of Mosul, in present-day Iraq. He was schooled by many prominent scholars of the era and worked as a merchant and teacher at the Umayyad Mosque in Damascus, before moving to Egypt in 1359 shortly before his death.

Al-Durayhim was a prolific writer, publishing more than 80 works in his short life, including a poem on cryptanalysis, a work on the rules of cryptology. His masterwork on cryptography, *Idah al-Mubham all al-mutar am*, was lost but he rewrote what he could recall from memory in a work called *Miftah al-kunuz li-idah al-marmuz* (Keys to Treasures Clarifying Ciphers). The book is broken down into five parts, covering essentials of cryptanalysis, encipherment methods, morphology of the Arabic alphabets (such as which letters can be combined), documentation of al-Kindi's frequency analysis and practical examples.

The coverage of encipherment methods provides an excellent overview of the state of cryptology at the time and it covers a range of transposition and substitution ciphers.

Durayhim's transposition methods include details of route ciphers. The work also reveals that Durayhim was aware of the principles of polyalphabetic substitution. His substitution tables are similar to those independently described by Vigenère (see page 69) and some scholars claim that Durayhim or perhaps al-Kindi may have been the first to recognize the power of the technique. Duryahim also outlines an encryption technique for replacing letters with numbers. Here is an example, using the Latin alphabet.

A	B	C	D	E	F	G	H	I
1	2	3	4	5	6	7	8	9
J	K	L	M	N	O	P	Q	R
10	20	30	40	50	60	70	80	90
S	T	U	V	W	X	Y	Z	
100	200	300	400	500	600	700	800	

Say we want to encode the word 'LETTER': this could be encrypted at a simple level as 30, 5, 200, 200, 5, 90.

However, the system can also be extended by rewriting these numbers as sums of two other figures and then re-encrypting. For example: 20 + 10, 2 + 3, 100 + 100, 100 + 100, 1 + 4, 40 + 50 which could be written as 20, 10, 2, 3, 100, 100, 100, 100, 1, 4, 40, 50 or, by reusing the table in reverse, could be encrypted as KJBCSSSSADMN. As long as the recipient knows the mathematical rule used, decryption is easy. Durayhim's treatise concludes with practical examples of frequency analysis.

It is unclear how much of Durayhim's work was original but as a chronicler he was first class, bringing together the ideas of other Arabic cryptographers such as al-Kindi, Ibn Adlan and Ibn Dunaynir.

As Dr. Mrayati says in his analysis of Duryahim's work, 'Ibn al-Durayhim's originality manifested itself first and foremost in his explanation and analysis of ciphering methods, their individual capabilities and qualifications, especially the substitution cipher. His originality was more evident in cryptography than cryptanalysis.'

Our knowledge of Durayhim's work comes largely from the encyclopedic masterpiece *Subh al-a'shá* (Dawn for the Blind), which was compiled by the Egyptian scholar Ahmad al-Qalqashandi in the mid-fourteenth century. The 14-volume work includes rich histories of Egypt and Syria as well as discussions of calligraphy and administration, as well as cryptology.

These show that the Middle East was the global focus for cryptography at the time and that their methods were without parallel.

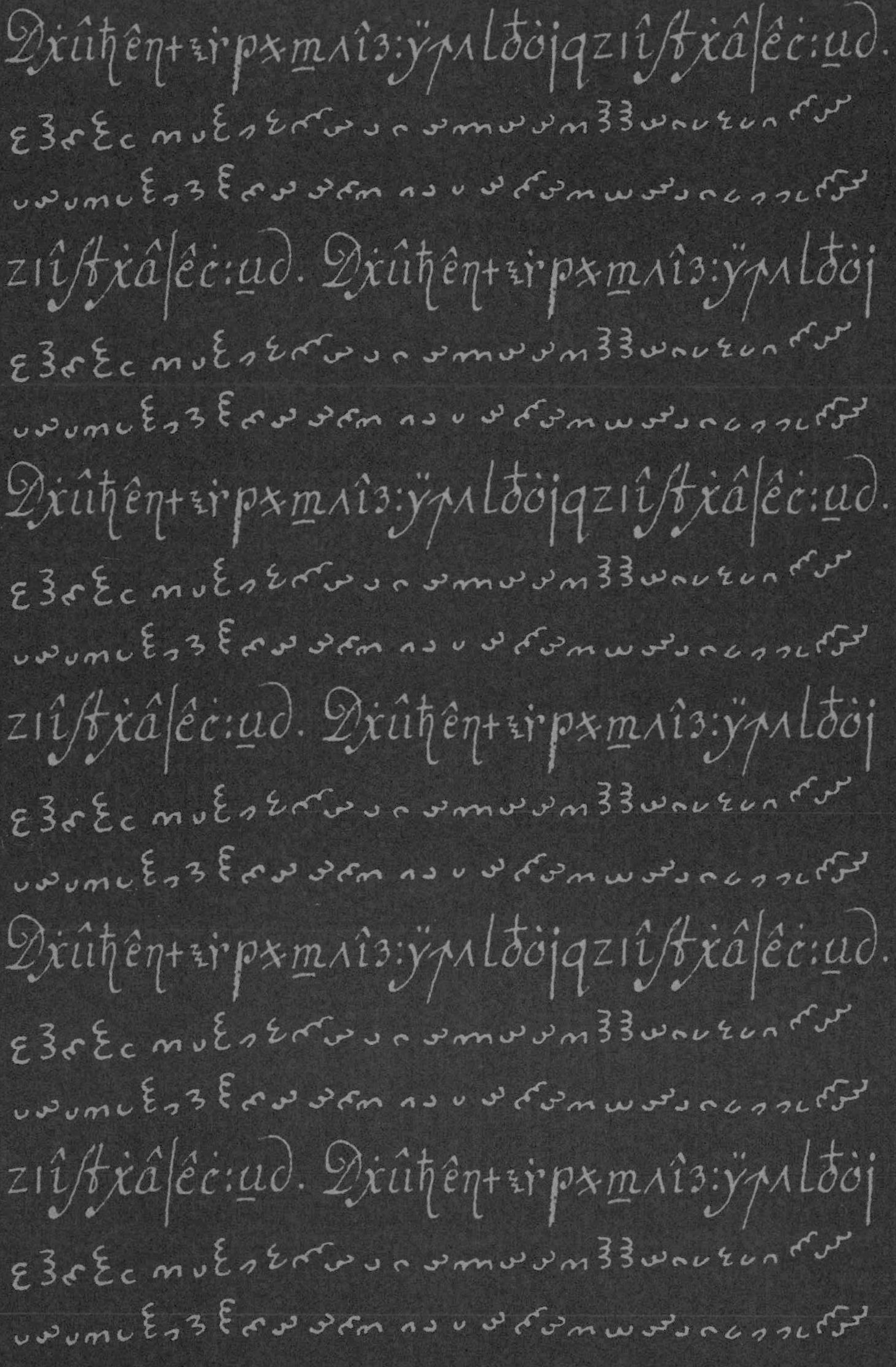

3 BEYOND THE ALPHABET

KEYS AND MULTIPLE ALPHABETS

The simple substitution ciphers that had served kings, religious leaders and the military for centuries started to look less secure during the second millennium CE, as codebreakers began to understand the power of al-Kindi's frequency analysis for revealing hidden messages. It meant that those wishing to encrypt messages needed to find ways of masking the telltale linguistic tracks that aided easy decipherment. This led to new techniques involving the use of multiple ciphertext symbols for single characters in plaintext messages and the introduction of more than one substitution alphabet when encrypting a message. This suddenly made the codebreaker's challenge considerably harder.

This period also saw one of the biggest improvements in security: using a key – a word or phrase – to establish the initial starting position of a cipher. Not knowing the key put cryptanalysts at a huge disadvantage. And a key that had to be generated from the plaintext message itself made the codebreaker's job infinitely harder.

Despite the increasing professionalism of the codebreaker's art, a number of messages, inscriptions and techniques from this period of history have resisted all attempts to decipher them.

N-gram Analysis

The technique of frequency analysis (see pages 30–35) is sometimes insufficient for cracking a cipher. This may be because the ciphertext is not long enough or is not representative of the distribution of letter frequency in the chosen language. Sometimes the codebreaker needs to look more closely at the text, and this is where n-gram analysis comes into play.

An n-gram is a sequence that is n letters, syllables, or words long. For example, a two-gram or bigram is two characters or words long. This might mean two-letter combinations (often called digraphs), such as **TH** or **EE**, two-syllable combinations, such as **EN-TION** or **ATE-LY** or two-word combinations such as **AFTER THE** or **LESS THAN**.

How does this help? In the same way that we analyze a ciphertext in order to find individual letters that represent **E, T, A** and so on, we can also analyze all the n-grams in a ciphertext and compare their frequencies with a database of n-grams taken from a corpus of text in the suspected language. The following chart, for example, shows an analysis of the frequency of appearance of digraphs in a corpus or database of 40,000 words carried out by Cornell University.

It shows that the most common digraphs in English are **TH, HE, IN** and **ER**. Note that the corpus chosen can yield variation in the order of these.The most common trigraphs in English, according to Northwest Nazarene physics professor William Packard are **THE, AND, THA, ENT, ION, TIO, FOR, NDE, HAS, NCE, TUS, OFT** and **MEN**. Another useful crib is the most commonly occurring double letters in English (**SS, EE, TT, FF, LL, MM** and **OO**) and the most common two- and three-letter words.

In order to use this knowledge in practice, consider the following ciphertext message: **BASH SH MAYB QYVGH BSQG BCYNGT FZHHSWTG BAG DTXE OYFYOSBZC**. The first action is to use the frequency analysis of individual letters. It is evident that the most common ciphertext letter is **B**, followed by **G**. If this text had the same distribution as standard text, we would make the assumption that **B** represents 'e' in plaintext and **G** represents 't'. This is possible, but it is not enough.

Frequency of digraphs in English

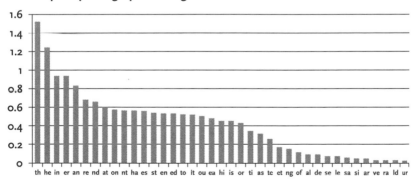

Looking more closely reveals one occurrence of a double letter – **HH**. It is already known that the most common double letter in the English language is 'ss'. So it is possible the the **H** in ciphertext stands for 's' in plaintext. If this is the case, when looking at the first two words of the ciphertext – **BASH SH** – it is reasonable to assume that **S** stands either for 'a' or 'i'.

Now consider the ciphertext word **BAG**. The only three-letter word in the message, this is most likely to be the word 'the,' the most common three-letter word in the English language. If this is true, then the first word would be 'this' or 'thas'. Using our options for the ciphertext letter **S**, 'this is' looks very promising so we assume that ciphertext **S** is plaintext 'i'. If we substitute what we already have we get: **THIS IS MHYT QYVES TIQE TCYNET FZSSIWTE THE DTXE OYFYOITZC.**

What about ciphertext **Y**? Using the letter 'a', which occurs with high frequency in English texts results in: **THIS IS MHAT QAVES TIQE TCANET FZSSIWTE THE DTXE OAFAOITZC.** What a cryptanalyst might do now is look at the letter patterns in words where letters remain unsolved. Anyone who does crosswords on a regular basis will be familiar with the process.

Take that last word: **OAFAOITZC**. There is only one English word that has this pattern of letters and a repeated letter at positions one and five – 'capacitor'. This gives us four more correspondences **O**, **F**, **Z**, and **C** are 'c,' 'p,' 'o' and 'r'. The ciphertext now reads: **THIS IS MHAT QAVES TIQE TRANET POSSIWTE THE DTXE CAPACITOR.** Continuing in this vein reveals 'possible' and then 'travel'. The word 'time' is then a good option from those available, suggesting the previous word is 'makes'. The word 'Mhat' can only be 'what'. That just leaves us **DTXE**, which is hard to deduce with such a short ciphertext. Fans of the movie *Back to the Future* will know that the missing word is 'flux', and the sentence is: **THIS IS WHAT MAKES TIME TRAVEL POSSIBLE THE FLUX CAPACITOR.**

Cryptanalysis is very much a matter of chiselling away using various techniques and seeing what works. Computerization has helped with some of the labourious tasks, such as analysis of digraph frequency, but a lot of it is still making guesses and trial and error. There are also more methodical methods of using n-gram analysis, such as Jakobsen's 'fast' method for breaking substitution ciphers. It is considered fast because the ciphertext only needs to be analyzed once to produce a frequency analysis histogram and a grid showing the frequency of appearance of digraphs. Jakobsen showed that the rows and columns of this digraph frequency grid can be swapped and compared with the frequency grid for standard English iteratively until the 'best' solution is found. The method works exceptionally well with monoalphabetic ciphers and also works very well with polyalphabetic ciphers which use a small number of alphabets.

Sitting somewhere between frequency analysis and n-gram analysis is a cryptanalytical technique known as contact analysis. Instead of looking at the frequency of individual letters, contact analysis considers the frequency with which certain letters appear next to others in a particular language.

For example, in English the letter 'u' follows the letter 'q' more than 99 percent of the time – the rest are occasions when you use words such as Iraq and it is followed by a space. We also know that 'v' is followed by 'e' more than two thirds of the time in English and 'h' by 'e' 46 percent of the time. Tables showing these values are available on the web.

To use this idea for cryptanalysis, you would create a similar table for all of the characters in your ciphertext alphabet. The rows and columns would be jumbled up but you start by identifying certain high probabilities – that 'q' will almost certainly be followed by 'u' and that 't' is very often followed by 'h' and 'k' by 'e'.

ALBERTI CIPHER DISC

A fifteenth-century innovation allowed the use of multiple alphabets to hide a message. The invention helped make the science of frequency analysis less potent.

For many centuries following Julius Caesar, cryptologists used simple substitution ciphers to hide their messages. Yet the work of al-Kindi showed that monoalphabetic substitution ciphers were vulnerable to the application of frequency analysis (see pages 30–35).

One of the first documented polyalphabetic ciphers was invented by Leon Battista Alberti, a Renaissance polymath. His great work on cryptography *De Cifris* was published in 1467. In it, he describes a device he called the 'formula,' a cipher wheel comprising two discs, one fixed (called the *stabilis*) and one moving (called the *mobilis*).

Leon Battista Alberti, a renaissance polymath and one of the earliest pioneers of polyalphabetic ciphers.

The outer stabilis is divided into 24 sections and marked into these are 20 letters of the Latin alphabet in red upper case in alphabetical order (aspirant 'h' and the rarely used 'k' and 'y' are not used). The remaining sections are numbered 1, 2, 3 and 4 in black. The inner mobilis shows all 23 Latin letters in lower case with the addition of the ampersand (&) in no particular order.

An enhanced version of this cipher disc was used in the American Civil War. Known as the Union Cipher Disc, it allowed soldiers to convert both letters and common word endings into strings of the digits one and eight.

Using the cipher

To use Alberti's device, both sender and recipient need a cipher wheel, in which the order of the letters on the inner mobilis is identical. The sender and recipient establish an index letter – say 'r'. The sender then looks at the letter in the stabilis that sits adjacent to 'r' on the mobilis – F in the example below – and writes uppercase **F** to start the ciphertext. The disc is now set, and the sender encrypts a few words or sentences in this position by finding the plaintext uppercase letter on the stabilis and writing down the lowercase plaintext character from the mobilis.

Using this method to encrypt the message 'all steps of learning must be found in nature' yields the first four words as **Fgzz qipsq yr zpgmxvxt** (remember that the first **F** merely shows the initial position of the index character 'r').

The sender can rotate the inner disc to a new position at any time. In the example shown below, the index letter 'r' now sits adjacent to the letter **M**. The sender writes uppercase **M** to signal this new position before continuing to encrypt the remaining words as **Mroys ag kvote nt tbsoxg**. (Note that we have used a 'v' for a 'u' in our message in English.)

In order to decrypt the message, the recipient simply reverses the procedure using the uppercase letters as a signal to set the disc to a new position.

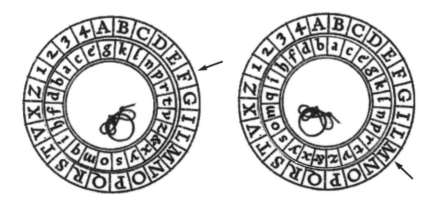

CARDAN GRILLES

Known to have been used by Francis Bacon and Cardinal Richelieu, these devices provide a mechanical way of concealing text within a longer message.

Girolamo Cardano (often known as Jerome Cardan) was a 16th century Italian polymath with interests in astrology, mathematics and medicine. He was born in Pavia, Italy in 1501 and during his life published over 100 books, including *Liber de ludo aleae* (*The Book of Games of Chance*), one of the first ever treatments of probability. Two of his many publications were on the subject of cryptography: *De Subtilitate* in 1550 and *De Rerum Varietate* in 1556. His name is known for a steganographic device called a Cardan grille.

Despite their relatively simple mode of operation, the difficulty in discovering the hidden messages meant that Cardan grilles remained in use long after Cardano died in 1576.

Using the cipher

A Cardan grille is a sheet of cardboard, wood, metal or other stiff material that has holes cut into it at irregular locations, such as in the simplified example right. The user places the grille

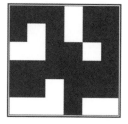

W	I	L	L	Y	O
U	E	A	T	S	O
M	E	N	I	G	H
T	A	T	S	A	M
S	R	O	O	M	D
E	A	R	O	L	Y

on a sheet of paper and writes out the message to be hidden in the holes – which in this case is the name 'Leonardo'.

The grille is then removed and the writer writes a longer message that incorporates these letters; here we have used 'Will you eat some night at Sam's room dear Oly'.

The recipient of the message must then have an identical grille to the sender so that when they place it on the longer message, the hidden message is revealed.

Cardano's grilles did not just use holes for individual letters but also groups of letters, as shown in the images below.

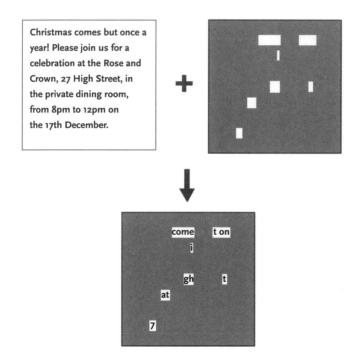

The message 'Come tonight at 7', hidden by Cardan grille.

Bellaso Cipher

In the 15th and 16th centuries, cryptologists began to recognize the power of using more than one alphabet in their ciphers.

The Italian cryptographer Giovan Battista Bellaso, born in Brescia in 1505, was a skilled cryptographer whose methods were used by both cardinals and counts during the Renaissance period.

His most important works were *La Cifra del Sig. Giovan Battista Bellaso*, published in 1553, and *Novi et singolari modi di cifrare*, published in 1555, which continued the work of the earlier volume. Bellaso built on the earlier use of polyalphabetic ciphers by the Abbot Trithemius (see page 66) by introducing the additional concept of employing a key, which would make cracking messages even harder.

As with other polyalphabetic ciphers, the way to crack them is to use Kasiski's method (see page 122), which breaks the ciphertext down by first working out how many cipher alphabets have been used and subsequently applying frequency analysis on each portion of the text.

Using the cipher

Bellaso's 1553 method uses eleven alphabets as shown in the top image on page 59. Note that at the time, the letters J, K and W were not used while the letter U and V were interchangeable. The shifts of the lower half-alphabets look random but are actually in a sequence so they can be learned by heart and reproduced without reference to the original book.

If you follow the sequence **A, E, I, O, V, C, G, M, Q, S, Y** and find this letter in the two letters at the left-hand side, you can see that the bottom row is shifted by one character compared to the previous one.

To use the cipher, a word or phrase must be agreed in advance between the sender and recipient. Bellaso called this a countersign, but it is now more commonly known as a key. The letters of the countersign are written out as many times as necessary above the letters of plaintext to be encrypted (see below). In the following example, the countersign is **FRANCE**. We write this countersign out as many times as needed so there is one letter for every letter of the plaintext. To encipher each letter, we look at the countersign letter and find it among the groups of two index letters at the left hand side of Bellaso's chart. We then look to find the plaintext letter in the alphabet next to those index letters and write down the letter that sits above or below that plaintext character. The recipient, already equipped with the countersign, simply does the operation in reverse to reveal the plaintext.

In his 1555 book, Bellaso suggested the use of different encryption alphabets for different recipients using popular phrases to create the encryption matrix. In this example he has used a line from Virgil's Aeneid to create the table: ARMA UIRUMQUE CANO TROIE QUI PRIMUS AB ORIS. He has first discarded the vowels and then

AB	a	b	c	d	e	f	g	h	i	l	m
	n	o	p	q	r	s	t	u	x	y	z
CD	a	b	c	d	e	f	g	h	i	l	m
	t	u	x	y	z	n	o	p	q	r	s
EF	a	b	c	d	e	f	g	h	i	l	m
	z	n	o	p	q	r	s	t	u	x	y
GH	a	b	c	d	e	f	g	h	i	l	m
	s	t	u	x	y	z	n	o	p	q	r
IL	a	b	c	d	e	f	g	h	i	l	m
	y	z	n	o	p	q	r	s	t	u	x
MN	a	b	c	d	e	f	g	h	i	l	m
	r	s	t	u	x	y	z	n	o	p	q
OP	a	b	c	d	e	f	g	h	i	l	m
	x	y	z	n	o	p	q	r	s	t	u
QR	a	b	c	d	e	f	g	h	i	l	m
	q	r	s	t	u	x	y	z	n	o	p
ST	a	b	c	d	e	f	g	h	i	l	m
	p	q	r	s	t	u	x	y	z	n	o
VX	a	b	c	d	e	f	g	h	i	l	m
	u	x	y	z	n	o	p	q	r	s	t
YZ	a	b	c	d	e	f	g	h	i	l	m
	o	p	q	r	s	t	u	x	y	z	n

Countersign	F	R	A	N	C	E	F	R	A	N	C	E	F	R	A	N	C	E	F	R
Plaintext	t	h	e	s	i	e	g	e	o	f	t	r	o	y	i	s	o	v	e	r
Ciphertext	H	Z	R	B	Q	Q	S	V	B	Y	A	F	C	G	X	B	G	I	Q	B

written down the consonants but only the first time they appear. Unused consonants are then appended to this alphabetically. The line from the Aeneid thus becomes RMQCNTPSB DFGHLXYZ.

Bellaso uses this string of letters in two ways. First he intersperses the vowels in the order AVIEO after the first five consonants to get RAMVQICENOTPSB DFGHLXYZ. These are split into pairs to get the index letters on the left hand side.

Then he takes the consonant string again and intersperses the vowels after every third consonant to get RMQACNTVPSBIDFGEHLXOYZ. He splits this into two halves to make the first encryption alphabet (shown next to index letters RA). For subsequent index letters, the bottom half is shifted one letter to the right. The encryption is carried out as in the previous example.

In 1564, Bellaso published *Il vero modo di scrivere in cifra* in which he extended his cipher into new areas with the introduction of the autokey cipher. With this, rather than agreeing a countersign between the sender and recipient, the plaintext itself is used.

RA	r	m	q	a	c	n	t	v	p	s	b
	i	d	f	g	e	h	l	x	o	y	z
MV	r	m	q	a	c	n	t	v	p	s	b
	z	i	d	f	g	e	h	l	x	o	y
QI	r	m	q	a	c	n	t	v	p	s	b
	y	z	i	d	f	g	e	h	l	x	o
CE	r	m	q	a	c	n	t	v	p	s	b
	o	y	z	i	d	f	g	e	h	l	x
NO	r	m	q	a	c	n	t	v	p	s	b
	x	o	y	z	i	d	f	g	e	h	l
TP	r	m	q	a	c	n	t	v	p	s	b
	l	x	o	y	z	i	d	f	g	e	h
SB	r	m	q	a	c	n	t	v	p	s	b
	h	l	x	o	y	z	i	d	f	g	e
DF	r	m	q	a	c	n	t	v	p	s	b
	e	h	l	x	o	y	z	i	d	f	g
GH	r	m	q	a	c	n	t	v	p	s	b
	g	e	h	l	x	o	y	z	i	d	f
LX	r	m	q	a	c	n	t	v	p	s	b
	f	g	e	h	l	x	o	y	z	i	d
YZ	r	m	q	a	c	n	t	v	p	s	b
	d	f	g	e	h	l	x	o	y	z	i

The Italian cryptographer Giovan Battista Bellaso generated this table from the line, 'arma uirumque cano troie qui.'

The autokey used five ciphertext alphabets as shown below and works as follows. To encrypt the phrase *'aue maria gratia plena'*, start with the top alphabet marked **IDVQ** and use it to encrypt the first letter of the plaintext, so that 'a' is encrypted as **M**. Cycle through the alphabets using them to encrypt subsequent letters until reaching the end of the first word – here, the 'u' is encrypted using the **OFER** alphabet (giving '**o**'), and the 'e' using the **AGMS** alphabet (giving '**B**').

Now use the initial letter of the first plaintext to choose the starting alphabet for the second word. Since '*aue*' begins with 'a', use the **AGMS** alphabet to encrypt the first letter of '*maria*'. Subsequent letters of the second word are then encrypted by cycling through the alphabets again. Continuing in the same manner, encrypting words starting with the alphabet indicated by the initial letter of the previous word, the message itself provides the key that gives the cipher its name. Once fully encrypted, the ciphertext reads: **MOB CXIUE QLTHXU FRDBE.**

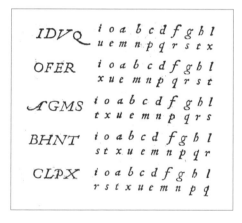

Ballaso's 1564 ciphertext table, detailing a method of ciphering messages using multiple alphabets.

Mantua Cipher

It took centuries for someone to come up with a cipher that could withstand al-Kindi's frequency analysis. The Mantua cipher, first seen in 1401, is the first documented use of homophonic substitution and its principles are still in use today.

Homophones are words that sound the same but are written differently, such as 'bear' and 'bare' or 'here' and 'hear'. A homophonic substitution cipher uses more than one ciphertext symbol to represent each plaintext letter. While monoalphabetic substitution ciphers are based on a one-to-one mapping between plaintext and ciphertext, homophonic substitution ciphers are many-to-one.

The use of homophones means that the distribution of letters in the ciphertext is disguised. Nonetheless, there are still ways of working out what is going on, by using n-gram analysis (see pages 50–55) and digraph and trigraph analysis in particular. This is because, even though the individual letter frequencies are disguised, those of digraphs and trigraphs are less well hidden. It is also possible to look for frequently occurring words. Knowing that 'the' is the most common word in the English language means that, with a long enough ciphertext, there is likely to be a repetition of a ciphertext sequence, even if homophones have been used.

One avenue of attack is to look for the digraph 'qu'. In English, the letter 'q' is almost always followed by the letter 'u'. The infrequency of 'q' in English means that it is only likely to be represented by a single ciphertext character. By analyzing a ciphertext to find a symbol that is only ever followed by two or three other symbols, it is possible to find 'q'.

Another popular method of homophonic substitution is to use two-digit numbers rather than letters and symbols (see page 64). The number of homophones is as close to proportional to the frequency in English as it is possible to get with a 100-cipher alphabet. Using this, 'the da Vinci code' could be encrypted as 69 65 41 48 20 82 51 77 66 96 23 09 13 89. (Note that

Frequency of letters in English

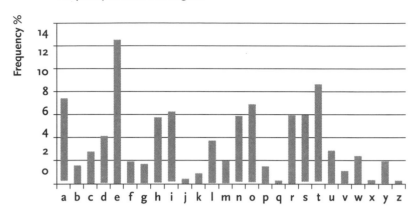

Frequency of letters in ciphertext

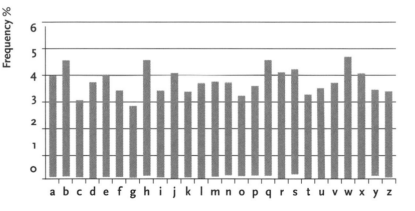

any of the two-digit homophone ciphers for a given letter may be used – the final 'e' could have been any one of the 12 different homophones listed.) Returning to the letter 'q', if using the two-digit homophonic alphabet above, any occurrences of 42 might be followed by 21, 67 or 92, but not by any other number. This would create opportunities for further analysis of word patterns.

Plaintext	a	b	c	d	e	f	g	h	i	j	k	l	m	n	o	p	q	r	s	t	u	v	w	x	y	z
Ciphertext	20	10	23	13	15	11	33	04	05	57	61	12	16	02	09	03	42	01	18	00	21	82	08	55	87	17
	22	85	50	30	24	70	68	06	51			44	26	35	14	72		19	28	07	67		81		99	
	31		66	48	27			38	76			56		59	25			29	49	34	92					
	32			94	40			65	80			95		60	39			37	83	36						
	47				41			78	96					77	43			71	86	58						
	53				45			91	98					90	52			79	88	64						
	73				46									97	62					69						
					54										75					93						
					63																					
					74																					
					84																					
					89																					

Using the cipher

The main reason for using homophones is to thwart the technique of frequency analysis (see pages 30–35) by flattening out the frequency histogram so that it looks like the one on page 63. A codebreaker would find it far more difficult to attack a ciphertext whose frequency analysis looks like this, because the most common letters are very difficult to pick out.

Instead of using single substitutions for each letter in the plaintext, a homophonic cipher involves having more substitutions for the most popular letters – often using numbers and punctuation symbols. The technique was first documented in 1401 in a piece of correspondence between the Duchy of Mantua and Simeone de Crema. In this, the writer reversed the usual order of the letters of the alphabet and added homophones for the vowels (see opposite):

More sophisticated homophonic ciphers flatten out the frequency histogram even farther than the Mantua cipher by using extra symbols for the most popular letters, not just the vowels. Each time a popular letter is encrypted any one of the possible ciphertext options is used. Thus, using the example above the plaintext message 'delete the files we have been infiltrated' becomes **5PHRAW ;N4 CDT7F ¥% SK©> 3+PJ MUCXH"BZ!R?** Removing the spaces between words would make it even harder to crack.

Plaintext	a	b	c	d	e	f	g	h	i	j	k	l	m	n	o	p	q	r	s	t	u	v	w	x	y	z
Ciphertext	K	3	#	5	P	C	Q	N	D	G	O	H	I	J	Y	E	L	B	F	A	[	©	¥	]	½	:
	Z			?	R			S	M			T		U	2			9	=	;						
	1				W			$	X					V	8			<	)	"						
	6				4			~	o					€	(			/	^	!						
	£				7				&						☆					\						
					%																					
					>																					
					+																					

AVE MARIA CIPHER

The German abbot Johannes Trithemius was the author of the first printed book on cryptography. Many misunderstood the content of the books he published, which were written in code, and he was accused of dealing with the Devil.

A snowstorm led to the publication of the first printed book on cryptography. Johannes Trithemius was on a journey between his university in Heidelberg and his home town of Trittenheim, when a blizzard forced him to seek cover in the abbey of St Martin in Spanheim. He was so taken by the monastic life that, after the snowstorm had passed and he was able to return home, he decided to enter the novitiate. Trithemius quickly rose to the role of abbot. At St Martin, he devoted many of his energies to writing, compiling a comprehensive list of theological works as well as a hugely successful book of Latin sermons. However, some of his writings were to see him forced to leave his post.

In 1499, he wrote a book called *Steganographia* which, even though a printed version was not available until 1606, seemed to deal with angels and magic. In fact, this magic was a cover for his writings on cryptography, but many believed he was dabbling with the Devil's works and he was forced to resign. Another of his cryptographic books, *Polygraphia*, was written in 1506 and published posthumously in 1518. With such an early date, it can claim to be the earliest printed book on cryptography.

The cipher that caused Trithemius problems in his role as abbot at St. Martin has become known as the Ave Maria cipher. As well as Ave Maria, Trithemius came up with a powerful method of using multiple alphabets.

Codebreakers rely on a number of shortcuts when deciding which method of encryption has been used. A well-read cryptanalyst of today would immediately assume that a passage of Latin religious text is likely to have been encrypted using the Ave Maria cipher. Such knowledge renders the ciphertext vulnerable to anyone who has access to a copy of *Polygraphia*. However, in Trithemius's era, few would have had access to the book or even have known of its existence, making the cipher highly secure.

For those working without *Polygraphia*, another method is required. The Ave Maria cipher is a polyalphabetic substitution cipher – even though the substitutions are words rather than individual letters. Using the standard method for attacking polyalphabetic ciphers (see page 128) – the first action is to analyze the text to reveal the number of alphabets used and then decode it using frequency analysis (see pages 30–35).

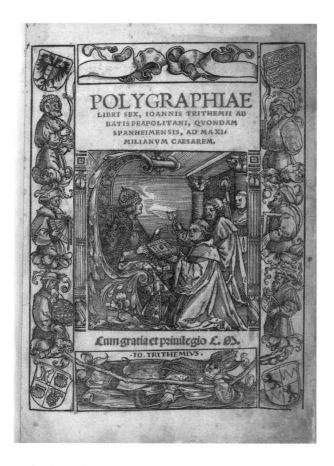

The cover of Trithemius' book Polygraphia, *which published posthumously in 1518. The engraving shows monks bearing keys – very apt considering the book's subject matter.*

Using the cipher

Trithemius's masterwork *Polygraphia*, a copy of which is on display at the National Cryptologic Museum outside Baltimore in Maryland, consists of 384 columns of letters of the alphabet, each with a corresponding codeword as shown in the examples below.

Say you wish to encipher the word 'abbeys.' Using the tables in *Polygraphia*, you write down the corresponding word for each letter in consecutive columns:

A — DEUS

B — CLEMENTISSIMUS

B — AMENITATEM

E — SUPERCELESTEM

Y — FAMULIS

S — FELICITATE

This ciphertext would read:

DEUS CLEMENTISSIMUS AMENITATEM SUPERCELESTEM FAMULIS FELICITATE

The method is known as the Ave Maria cipher because the resulting ciphertext sounds like a prayer. The recipient of the coded message would look at the first word of the ciphertext and identify which column contained that word. By starting from that column they could then decrypt the entire message.

The cipher had one significant advantage. As prayers were ubiquitous in written texts of the period, the message sent had the appearance of being something commonplace, so while the cipher could be broken, it might not draw attention to itself. Modern cryptologists have turned to ordinary material such as spam email to achieve a similar result.

Vigenère Cipher

The French cryptographer Blaise de Vigenère is best known for a cipher that, for many years, was dubbed *le chiffre indéchiffrable*, the undecipherable cipher.

De Vigenère was another pioneer of the polyalphabetic cipher and gave his name to one of the best-known examples. In his book *Traicté des chiffres (Treatise on Ciphers)*, he demonstrated an early method of using multiple alphabets. As with Bellaso's, the alphabets are split in half (as below) but rather than using an autokey, as in Bellaso's later version, Vigenère's version sticks to using a previously agreed key.

Like some other polyalphabetic ciphers, it is susceptible to the Kasiski method (see page 122) in which the ciphertext is analyzed for repeating patterns in order to gain knowledge of the number of ciphertext alphabets used. A variant method of the Vigenère cipher, called the running key method, uses a key that is the same length as the plaintext message. This improvement means that the Kasiski method of observing repetitions no longer works.

A	a	b	c	d	e	f	g	h	i	l
B	m	n	o	p	q	r	s	t	u	x
C	a	b	c	d	e	f	g	h	i	l
D	x	m	n	o	p	q	r	s	t	u
E	a	b	c	d	e	f	g	h	i	l
F	u	x	m	n	o	p	q	r	s	t
G	a	b	c	d	e	f	g	h	i	l
H	t	u	x	m	n	o	p	q	r	s
I	a	b	c	d	e	f	g	h	i	l
L	s	t	u	x	m	n	o	p	q	r
M	a	b	c	d	e	f	g	h	i	l
N	r	s	t	u	x	m	n	o	p	q
O	a	b	c	d	e	f	g	h	i	l
P	q	r	s	t	u	x	m	n	o	p
Q	a	b	c	d	e	f	g	h	i	l
R	p	q	r	s	t	u	x	m	n	o
S	a	b	c	d	e	f	g	h	i	l
T	o	p	q	r	s	t	u	x	m	n
V	a	b	c	d	e	f	g	h	i	l
X	n	o	p	q	r	s	t	u	x	m

Using the cipher

Start with a key phrase and a plaintext message you wish to encrypt.
Vigenère gives the example of *le iour obscur* as the key and *au nom de
l'eternel soit mon commencement* as the plaintext.

You take each letter of the key in turn and look up the corresponding
alphabet in the table on page 69. The first letter of the key is 'l' so we
find that letter in the left most column. We then take the first letter of
the plaintext and find it in the alphabet in that section of the grid: the
adjacent letter is 's' so this becomes the first letter of the ciphertext. We
then move to the second letter of the key, the letter 'e', and find that
alphabet. We then use this to encrypt the second letter of the plaintext
'u' becomes 'a' in the ciphertext. When all of the key letters are used
up, you start again from the beginning.

Key	L	E	I	O	V	R	O	B	S	C	V	R	L	E	I	...
Plaintext	a	v	n	o	m	d	e	l	e	t	e	r	n	e	l	...
Ciphertext	S	A	F	I	L	S	U	X	S	I	R	C	F	O	R	...

Despite Bellaso's introduction of the countersign or key, the system is
known as a Vigenère cipher. Systems like these are effectively multiple
Caesar shifts – you can see that each row of the alphabet is shifted by
one more character than the previous one.

Vigenère ciphers are also susceptible to analysis of the index of
coincidence proposed by William F Friedman, a cryptographer who ran
the research department of the US Army's Signals Intelligence Service.
This method (see page 85) works by looking at the probability that the
same letter appears in the same position in two ciphertexts encrypted
using the same cipher alphabet.

The Vigenère square opposite, often known as a tabula recta,
shows how you might use the Vigenère cipher using the modern Latin
alphabet. Say we want to encrypt the plaintext 'the ship leaves at dawn.'
We choose a key, such as the name ROBERT, keep repeating the letters

	A	B	C	D	E	F	G	H	I	J	K	L	M	N	O	P	Q	R	S	T	U	V	W	X	Y	Z
A	A	B	C	D	E	F	G	H	I	J	K	L	M	N	O	P	Q	R	S	T	U	V	W	X	Y	Z
B	B	C	D	E	F	G	H	I	J	K	L	M	N	O	P	Q	R	S	T	U	V	W	X	Y	Z	A
C	C	D	E	F	G	H	I	J	K	L	M	N	O	P	Q	R	S	T	U	V	W	X	Y	Z	A	B
D	D	E	F	G	H	I	J	K	L	M	N	O	P	Q	R	S	T	U	V	W	X	Y	Z	A	B	C
E	E	F	G	H	I	J	K	L	M	N	O	P	Q	R	S	T	U	V	W	X	Y	Z	A	B	C	D
F	F	G	H	I	J	K	L	M	N	O	P	Q	R	S	T	U	V	W	X	Y	Z	A	B	C	D	E
G	G	H	I	J	K	L	M	N	O	P	Q	R	S	T	U	V	W	X	Y	Z	A	B	C	D	E	F
H	H	I	J	K	L	M	N	O	P	Q	R	S	T	U	V	W	X	Y	Z	A	B	C	D	E	F	G
I	I	J	K	L	M	N	O	P	Q	R	S	T	U	V	W	X	Y	Z	A	B	C	D	E	F	G	H
J	J	K	L	M	N	O	P	Q	R	S	T	U	V	W	X	Y	Z	A	B	C	D	E	F	G	H	I
K	K	L	M	N	O	P	Q	R	S	T	U	V	W	X	Y	Z	A	B	C	D	E	F	G	H	I	J
L	L	M	N	O	P	Q	R	S	T	U	V	W	X	Y	Z	A	B	C	D	E	F	G	H	I	J	K
M	M	N	O	P	Q	R	S	T	U	V	W	X	Y	Z	A	B	C	D	E	F	G	H	I	J	K	L
N	N	O	P	Q	R	S	T	U	V	W	X	Y	Z	A	B	C	D	E	F	G	H	I	J	K	L	M
O	O	P	Q	R	S	T	U	V	W	X	Y	Z	A	B	C	D	E	F	G	H	I	J	K	L	M	N
P	P	Q	R	S	T	U	V	W	X	Y	Z	A	B	C	D	E	F	G	H	I	J	K	L	M	N	O
Q	Q	R	S	T	U	V	W	X	Y	Z	A	B	C	D	E	F	G	H	I	J	K	L	M	N	O	P
R	R	S	T	U	V	W	X	Y	Z	A	B	C	D	E	F	G	H	I	J	K	L	M	N	O	P	Q
S	S	T	U	V	W	X	Y	Z	A	B	C	D	E	F	G	H	I	J	K	L	M	N	O	P	Q	R
T	T	U	V	W	X	Y	Z	A	B	C	D	E	F	G	H	I	J	K	L	M	N	O	P	Q	R	S
U	U	V	W	X	Y	Z	A	B	C	D	E	F	G	H	I	J	K	L	M	N	O	P	Q	R	S	T
V	V	W	X	Y	Z	A	B	C	D	E	F	G	H	I	J	K	L	M	N	O	P	Q	R	S	T	U
W	W	X	Y	Z	A	B	C	D	E	F	G	H	I	J	K	L	M	N	O	P	Q	R	S	T	U	V
X	X	Y	Z	A	B	C	D	E	F	G	H	I	J	K	L	M	N	O	P	Q	R	S	T	U	V	W
Y	Y	Z	A	B	C	D	E	F	G	H	I	J	K	L	M	N	O	P	Q	R	S	T	U	V	W	X
Z	Z	A	B	C	D	E	F	G	H	I	J	K	L	M	N	O	P	Q	R	S	T	U	V	W	X	Y

The tabula recta, also known as the Vignère square, was first used as a codebreaking tool by Johannes Trithemius in his book Polygraphia.

of the key and write the corresponding letter of the plaintext below. Using the tabula recta, we look up the row starting with the key letter and then move across to the column headed by the plaintext letter. The ciphertext is the letter at the intersection of these. This is shown in the example below, giving us the ciphertext **KVF WYBG ZFEMXJ OU HRPE**.

Key	R	O	B	E	R	T	R	O	B	E	R	T	R	O	B	E	R	T	R
Plaintext	t	h	e	s	h	i	p	l	e	a	v	e	s	a	t	d	a	w	n
Ciphertext	K	V	F	W	Y	B	G	Z	F	E	M	X	J	O	U	H	R	P	E

CODEBREAKERS OF HISTORY

ÉTIENNE BAZERIES

Cryptographic history is punctuated with cases in which an impressive new encryption method is invented only for it to languish unused in practice because of the difficulty in making it work quickly enough in the field.

The Vigenère cipher (see pages 69–71) is one such method – because it uses multiple alphabets, it is far more difficult to break than a monoalphabetic cipher, but this very fact makes it slow to use.

In the early seventeenth century, Antoine Rossignol demonstrated his expertise in the art of codebreaking by deciphering an encrypted letter taken from a messenger leaving the besieged city of Réalmont. The letter revealed that the Huguenots inside the city would be unable to hold on for much longer and, presented with the deciphered contents of the message, they soon surrendered to the French army.

Antoine Rossignol and his son Bonaventure were quickly employed by the French court for their skills. Their greatest achievement was the creation of an advanced encryption method called *Le Grand Chiffre* ('The Great Cipher').

The Rossignols' Great Cipher is what is known in cryptography as a

Antoine Rossignol, co-creator of the Grand Cipher, was employed by the French court in the seventeenth century for his codebreaking skills.

nomenclator. Nomenclators are a special form of homophonic substitution cipher (see pages 62–65). They get their name from the term used to describe a servant whose job it was to remember the names of people introduced to their master during political or social gatherings.

Nomenclator ciphers rely on using a code book that originally contained names – and, later, other common words or phrases – and a number of homophonic codewords that could be used in the place of those names, words, or phrases, in a message.

Thus a plaintext message of 'Meet with Christopher Taylor at 2.30 on Friday', could be rendered as MEET WITH 236422 AT 2.30 ON FRIDAY, where 236422 is one of a number of homophones chosen from the code book.

The Great Cipher was eventually broken by the nineteenth-century French army cryptologist Étienne Bazeries, one of the inventors of the cylindrical cryptograph. Bazeries analyzed five dispatches from Louis XIV dating from 1691. They contained around 11,000 numbers, of which 600 were different. (Note that other versions of the Great Cipher used different numbers of homophones – a weaker version used by the lower ranks was called *Le Petit Chiffre* and used 367 groups.)

Bazeries tried the common techniques of frequency analysis and n-gram analysis on the Great Cipher without success. It was only when he postulated that some of the ciphers represented syllables, as well as complete words, that he managed to uncover its secrets. He also discovered that some numbers meant 'ignore the previous number', making the code particularly fiendish. The Great Cipher uses codes for words such as 'quatre' but also for syllables such as 'mo' making it much harder to decipher.

The deciphering of the messages also revealed a possible solution to the mystery of the Man in the Iron Mask, a prisoner of Louis XIV who was forced to wear a black mask and whose identity has long been a matter for speculation. Bazeries interpreted one of the messages as an identification of the prisoner as General Vivien de Bulonde, whom Louis XIV had imprisoned for his role in the Siege of Cuneo.

SHUGBOROUGH INSCRIPTION

A short inscription on an eighteenth-century monument in the garden of an English country house might hold the secret of the final resting place of the elusive Holy Grail – if only the inscription could be deciphered.

Shugborough is a Georgian mansion house in Staffordshire in England's West Midlands, and the ancestral home of the Earl of Lichfield. The estate's nationally important and protected gardens are home to eight monuments, one of which is linked to the legend of the Holy Grail, the cup supposed to have been used by Jesus to serve wine at the Last Supper.

The Shepherd's Monument, carved in marble and standing 300 centimetres (10 feet) high, dates from around 1748. The monument, set within a rustic arch, depicts a mirror image of leading French Baroque painter Nicola Poussin's work *Shepherds of Arcadia*, which itself dates from 1637–1638. It was sculpted by the Flemish artist Peter Scheemakers following a commission by Shugborough's owner Thomas Anson. Both Anson and Poussin are thought to have belonged to secret societies, possibly the Priory of Sion, the successor to the Knights Templar.

A close-up of the monument showing the shepherd's hand pointing to an undeciphered inscription. One theory is that the inscription reveals the location of the Holy Grail.

Another supposed connection was proposed in the 1982 book *The Holy Blood and the Holy Grail*, which noted that one of the shepherds is pointing to an inscription on a tomb showing the words *Et in Arcadia Ego*. The authors argue that the phrase is an anagram of *I Tego arcana dei* which translates as 'Begone! I keep God's secrets', which they propose relates to the final resting place of Jesus or another figure from the Bible. The suggestion is that by revealing Shugborough's message, this place may be found.

The code itself is a series of ten letters: 'O.U.O.S.V.A.V.V.' on one line, with 'D.' and 'M.' in the right and left hand corners below. The main challenge for codebreakers is the brevity of the ciphertext, which rules out most conventional methods of cracking it. Charles Darwin and Charles Dickens both tried to solve it, but failed.

That the letters D.M. appear on a separate line is probably significant. Many believe that these letters stand for the Latin phrase *Dis Manibus*, which often appears on Roman tombs. It means 'for the Manes': Manes is the name given to a group of deities that represent the lost souls of loved ones.

Shugborough Estate eventually called in codebreakers who worked at World War II codebreaking centre Bletchley Park for their views on the inscription. One unnamed American professional codebreaker employed various cryptanalytical techniques on the inscription. He is said to have noticed one possible substitution, the sequence SEJ, which he suggested might be the first three letters of Jesus reversed. With this substitution, the inscription revealed the message 'Jesus h defy' and the codebreaker suggested that the H actually stood for the Greek letter *chi*, often used to represent Christ. His interpretation was that the inscription could be a Templar message denying the divinity of Christ. The full details of the method have not been revealed, making it hard for other codebreakers to check the American's work.

However, there may be a more human answer to the riddle. Sheila Lawn, who worked at Bletchley Park, believes the message is one of love and is an abbreviation for the Latin phrase *Optima Uxoris Optima Sororis Viduus Amantissimus Vovit Virtutibus*, which means 'Best wife, Best sister, Widower most loving vows virtuously'.

ARNOLD CIPHER

The great traitor of America's War of Independence used
code to hide his correspondence with the British.

Benedict Arnold is well known as the traitor who defected to the
British side in the War of Independence , also known as the American
Revolutionary War. When the War of Independence began and the
Thirteen Colonies declared their independence from Great Britain, Arnold
led various campaigns against the British. Yet by 1779, he had decided to
switch allegiance and started corresponding in code with John André, the
adjutant to the commander-in-chief of British forces in North America.

In his secret communications, Arnold agreed to hand over the
strategically important fortifications at West Point to the British in
exchange for the sum of 20,000 pounds.

The British made their plans to take West Point but André was caught
on American soil with papers relating to the agreement and Arnold's
treachery was revealed. Arnold escaped to the safety of the British ship
Vulture, but André was tried as a spy and hanged.

Understanding the cipher

The method Arnold used to communicate with André is one of a class
called book ciphers that use standard books as the method of encryption.

One of Arnold's letters shows how the method works. Some words are
written out with encryption and every few words there is a string of three
numbers separated by dots. John André explained the technique in a 1779
letter to Benedict Arnold's agent Joseph Stansbury.

*'You leave me with a long book similar to yours. Three numbers make a
word. The first is the page, the second the line, the third the word. A comma
is placed between each word. When only the first letter of the line is wanted
in order to compose a Word not in the book, the number representing the
Word will be ╪ (unit with a stroke across).'*

Thus a string of 150.10.6 would mean that the recipient had to turn to the 150th page of the book, go to the tenth line and read the sixth word from the left.

Arnold and André both had identical copies of either Sir William Blackstone's *Commentaries on the Laws of England* or Nathan Bailey's *Universal Etymological Dictionary* in order to create their code and communicate their plans for West Point in secret.

To add to the obfuscation, the pair pretended to be merchants and occasionally left words relating to their supposed trade unencrypted so that anyone intercepting and reading the letters might believe it was purely business correspondence.

Using the cipher

Anyone hoping to decrypt the message must have a copy of the book used to encrypt it. Not only that, the book must be an identical copy – a different edition may have different pagination.

The advantage of using a standard book – that no special codebook has to be exchanged between sender and recipient – can also be a weakness. If someone intercepts a coded message and guesses which standard book has been used (dictionaries and the Bible are popular choices) the message can easily be read.

The cipher also has the problem that if number sequences are regularly reused, someone intercepting the message might be able to guess the encrypted word.

CODEBREAKERS OF HISTORY

KNIGHT, MEGYESI AND SCHAEFER

In the library of the German Academy of Science in Berlin there sits a book beautifully bound in green and gold, containing 105 pages of neat script. The only recognizable pieces of text are the inscriptions 'Philipp 1866' and 'Copiales 3'; the rest is clearly some form of cipher. The book itself dates from the early 1700s.

The Copiale cipher was deciphered by Kevin Knight of California's USC Information Sciences Institute and Beáta Megyesi and Christiane Schaefer of Uppsala University in Sweden. They used frequency analysis (see pages 30–35) to discover the most frequent symbol ('∧' which was used 412 times), and n-gram analysis (see pages 50–55) to discover the most common digraphs and trigraphs. Given the presence of Roman letters in the cipher, the researchers initially considered the possibility that the abstract symbols were nulls and removed them. After comparing the

An example of Copiale cipher in a book dating from the early 1700s. Apart from two recognizable pieces of text, the entirety of this book was written in cipher.

frequency analysis of the remaining text with forty languages, starting with German, they discarded this idea. The number of symbols then led the team to consider the possibility that a homophonic substitution cipher had been used (see pages 62–65). They chose German as the target language for three reasons: the book had been found in Germany, the earlier textual analysis gave a slight preference for German, and the 'Philipp' inscription used the German double-p form.

The team had also noticed that the Roman vowels often appeared with a circumflex over them and that, when they appeared in the ciphertext, they

78

were almost always preceded by a 'z' or 'ɪɪ' symbol and were frequently followed by two other symbols. By analyzing the frequency of digraphs and trigraphs in German, they postulated possible substitutions for the plaintext letters 'c,' 'h' and 't' and made the leap to the conclusion that the vowels with circumflexes all represented the plaintext letter 'e'. From these, they identified correspondences for fifty of the ninety ciphertext symbols.

The next big leap in cracking the Copiale cipher came from sections of text, such as the following, where the ? stands for as-yet undecrypted characters of different types: ?GEHEIMER? UNTERLIST? VOR? DIE? GESELLE? ERDER? TITEL? CEREMONIE? DER? AUFNAHME.

The language is clearly German and from this the cryptanalysts suddenly understood that the unaccented Roman letters in the ciphertext represented spaces. The team also realized that a colon did not represent a character as such, but merely indicated that the previous letter should be repeated. By looking at the partially decrypted words +AFLNER, +NUPFTUCHS and GESELL+AFT, they realized that the + symbol stood for 'sch'. The decrypted document was revealed to contain details of the initiation ceremony of the Oculists, a group of ophthalmologists led by Count Friedrich August von Veltheim. The book appears to detail Masonic rites. One section of the translated text (with some symbols marked '??' still unknown) reads: 'All those present members reach for the candles, place themselves around the candidate and the master of ceremonies ?? plucks a hair from the eyebrow with a pair of small tweezers under constant urging, comfort and encouragement.'

DORABELLA CIPHER

A short note written by composer Edward Elgar to
a woman twenty years his junior continues to keep
cryptanalysts guessing.

In July 1897, the English composer Elgar and his wife Alice were invited to
visit the Reverend Alfred Penny and his wife at Wolverhampton Rectory.
Following their stay, Elgar wrote a note of thanks to the family. Included
with the letter was a note intended for their 23-year-old daughter, Dora,
written in cipher, which has never been satisfactorily deciphered.

Understanding the cipher

The ciphertext comprises 87 characters in total, of which 24 are different.
Each symbol is made up of a series of connected semicircles, oriented in
one of eight directions. Dora herself claims never to have decoded any
hidden message and Elgar never revealed its contents. The note itself only
came to light when Dora wrote a book on his life in 1937. Elgar and Dora
remained friends until the composer died and he even named one of his
Enigma Variations in her honour, entitling it *Dorabella*.

One of the major challenges in breaking the Dorabella Cipher is its
brevity. The number of distinct symbols suggests that it is a simple
substitution cipher but, if so, the ciphertext is not long enough to succumb
to frequency analysis. Some codebreakers, including Javier Atance, believe
that the cipher is not writing at all, but rather a coded musical piece with
the orientations representing notes and the number of semicircles relating
to natural, flat and sharp notes.

Another challenge for the codebreaker is that Elgar regularly used
nonsense words, anagrams and unusual spellings in his own writings. One
of the most respected attempts at a solution was made by the musicologist
Eric Sams. In his 1970 *Musical Times* article *Elgar's Cipher Letter to
Dorabella*, Sams suggests that Elgar used a combination of substitution,
phonetics and Greek letters to hide his intended message. The logic is at

The Dorabella Cipher in Elgar's original hand. Dora herself claimed to not understand the message and the note has attracted numerous theories, none conclusive.

times tenuous but the proposed plaintext seems to make some sort of sense: 'Starts: Larks! It's chaotic, but a cloak obscures my new letters, A, B . . . Below: I own the dark makes E. E. sigh when you are too long gone.'

Sams went on to suggest that the Dorabella cipher was the key to the hidden theme of Elgar's *Enigma Variations*, which also remains stubbornly undiscovered. In 2007, the Elgar Society organized a Dorabella Cipher competition with a prize of £1,500 to mark the 150th anniversary of the composer's birth. None of the decryptions entered were considered sufficiently convincing to win.

There are other proposed decryptions, which suggest that Dorabella is a so-called pigpen cipher, in which letters are replaced by symbols representing their locations in a simple grid. This is supported by notes found in one of Elgar's notebooks from many years later. Although the same symbols are used in his notebook, they produce gibberish when the same system is used on the original Dorabella ciphertext. Tony Gaffney, writing under the pseudonym Jean Palmer, believes the message uses a pigpen cipher of this construction with substitutions. This, coupled with copious use of anagrams and phonetics, leads to the following, somewhat obscure, plaintext: 'B (Bella) hellcat i.e. war using ?? hens shells is why your antiquarian net diminishes hem sorry you theo oh 'tis God then me so la do e (Elgar) adieu'. Whether this solution, known as the Hellcat Solution, is the true message, is anyone's guess.

$$IC = c \times \left(\left(\frac{n_a}{N} \times \frac{n_a - 1}{N - 1} \right) + \left(\frac{n_b}{N} \times \frac{n_b - 1}{N - 1} \right) + \cdots + \left(\frac{n_z}{N} \times \frac{n_z - 1}{N - 1} \right) \right)$$

$$IC = c \times \left(\left(\frac{n_a}{N} \times \frac{n_a - 1}{N - 1} \right) + \left(\frac{n_b}{N} \times \frac{n_b - 1}{N - 1} \right) + \cdots + \left(\frac{n_z}{N} \times \frac{n_z - 1}{N - 1} \right) \right)$$

$$IC = c \times \left(\left(\frac{n_a}{N} \times \frac{n_a - 1}{N - 1} \right) + \left(\frac{n_b}{N} \times \frac{n_b - 1}{N - 1} \right) + \cdots + \left(\frac{n_z}{N} \times \frac{n_z - 1}{N - 1} \right) \right)$$

$$IC = c \times \left(\left(\frac{n_a}{N} \times \frac{n_a - 1}{N - 1} \right) + \left(\frac{n_b}{N} \times \frac{n_b \,\overset{o}{-} 1}{N - 1} \right) + \cdots + \left(\frac{n_z}{N} \times \frac{n_z - 1}{N - 1} \right) \right)$$

$$IC = c \times \left(\left(\frac{n_a}{N} \times \frac{n_a - 1}{N - 1} \right) + \left(\frac{n_b}{N} \times \frac{n_b - 1}{N - 1} \right) + \cdots + \left(\frac{n_z}{N} \times \frac{n_z - 1}{N - 1} \right) \right)$$

$$IC = c \times \left(\left(\frac{n_a}{N} \times \frac{n_a - 1}{N - 1} \right) + \left(\frac{n_b}{N} \times \frac{n_b - 1}{N - 1} \right) + \cdots + \left(\frac{n_z}{N} \times \frac{n_z - 1}{N - 1} \right) \right)$$

$$IC = c \times \left(\left(\frac{n_a}{N} \times \frac{n_a - 1}{N - 1} \right) + \left(\frac{n_b}{N} \times \frac{n_b - 1}{N - 1} \right) + \cdots + \left(\frac{n_z}{N} \times \frac{n_z - 1}{N - 1} \right) \right)$$

98C92   59C5   11311   1C392   10371   0302   21290   5181   39695
23571   17504   11289   18276   18101   0317   0228   17694   4473

$$C = c \times \left(\left(\frac{n_a}{N} \times \frac{n_a-1}{N-1} \right) + \left(\frac{n_b}{N} \times \frac{n_b-1}{N-1} \right) + \cdots + \left(\frac{n_z}{N} \times \frac{n_z-1}{N-1} \right) \right)$$

333   4725   4458   59C5   17166   13851   4458   17149   14471
3850   12224   6929   14991   7382   15857   67893   14218   36477

$$C = c \times \left(\left(\frac{n_a}{N} \times \frac{n_a-1}{N-1} \right) + \left(\frac{n_b}{N} \times \frac{n_b-1}{N-1} \right) + \cdots + \left(\frac{n_z}{N} \times \frac{n_z-1}{N-1} \right) \right)$$

98C92   59C5   11311   1C392   10371   0302   21290   5181   39695
23571   17504   11289   18276   18101   0317   0228   17694   4473

$$C = c \times \left(\left(\frac{n_a}{N} \times \frac{n_a-1}{N-1} \right) + \left(\frac{n_b}{N} \times \frac{n_b-1}{N-1} \right) + \cdots + \left(\frac{n_z}{N} \times \frac{n_z-1}{N-1} \right) \right)$$

333   4725   4458   59C5   17166   13851   4458   17149   14471
3850   12224   6929   14991   7382   15857   67893   14218   36477

$$C = c \times \left(\left(\frac{n_a}{N} \times \frac{n_a-1}{N-1} \right) + \left(\frac{n_b}{N} \times \frac{n_b-1}{N-1} \right) + \cdots + \left(\frac{n_z}{N} \times \frac{n_z-1}{N-1} \right) \right)$$

98C92
23571

$C = c$

4 THE AGE OF TELEGRAPHY

33
850

$= c$

8C92   59C5   11311   1C392   10371   0302   21290   5181   39695
3571   17504   11289   18276   18101   0317   0228   17694   4473

$$= c \times \left(\left(\frac{n_a}{N} \times \frac{n_a-1}{\rule{1cm}{0.3em}} \right) + \left(\frac{n_b}{N} \times \frac{n_b-1}{N-1} \right) + \cdots + \left(\frac{n_z}{N} \times \frac{n_z-1}{\rule{1cm}{0.3em}} \right) \right)$$

33   4725   4458   59C5   17166   13851   4458   17149   14471
850   12224   6929   14991   7382   15857   67893   14218   36477

ELECTRONIC CRYPTOGRAPHY

The cylindrical cryptograph invented by Thomas Jefferson – or, at least, popularized by the future third president of the United States – was probably the last gasp of cryptology's mechanical era. The device was relatively simple and used polyalphabetic ciphers, which had become essential to keeping messages secret. The Industrial Revolution of the late nineteenth century did not just bring change to the world of manufacturing and agriculture, however. The increasing importance of mechanization also brought significant advances in both cryptology and cryptanalysis. In some senses, the stakes had never been higher. Powerful navies ruled the seas and commerce was becoming increasingly global. Entrepreneurs recognized that fortunes were there for the making for those who were first to find and use market information.

The eighteenth and nineteenth centuries also saw the emergence of an understanding of electricity and magnetism and, eventually, through the work of Oersted, Ampère, Faraday and Maxwell, that the two were intricately linked in a single force of nature. The invention of the electric motor only hastened the pace of progress, meaning that people increasingly conducted business beyond their own backyards. The need to communicate in a secure manner became even more important.

The end of the nineteenth century and the start of the twentieth marked the beginning of the end for the amateur codebreaker, as some began to realize that there were ways of making ciphers practically unbreakable by anyone working on their own. At the time, the skills required by any good codebreaker centred on a great deal of patience – many codes that involved more than simple substitutions required a great deal of analysis and checking. Foreign languages were also important, especially in times of war, when an enemy's message is not in the codebreaker's mother tongue. Linguistic skills were particularly useful, because many of the ways in which codes are broken rely on suggesting candidate words and phrases. For some this linguistic skill needs to be historical rather than current. Many are the cases of relics whose inscriptions are written in alphabets and languages that have been lost or obscured in the mists of time.

As the electric telegraph crisscrossed the world and commercial codes became commonplace, mathematical skills became more crucial. Suddenly mathematicians were in demand as the world moved away from methods of creating ciphers using things such as lists of words in codebooks toward algorithms that work on the numerical representation of the letters themselves, twisting them in ways that would tax the cleverest of brains. The increasingly global nature of both trade and war saw the stakes involved in the battle between cryptologists and cryptanalysts raised to new levels.

The decrpytion of the so-called Zimmermann Telegram (see pages 114–117) changed the course of war in a way never seen before. While battle raged in the old world, America remained resolutely neutral until plans to carve up the United States and hand over territories to Mexico were revealed. The dominance of the mathematical approach escalated as the world's thoughts turned to war and the need for new methods of sending secure communication of sensitive and classified information became crucial. The invention of one-time pads – and the mathematical proof by Gilbert Vernam that, if used correctly, no one could break them – surely signaled the end of the art of cryptanalysis. Or did it?

Index of Coincidence

The index of coincidence is a measure of the probability that, when you take two random letters from a piece of text they are the same letter. If your text is N letters in length and the number of times the letter 'a', for example, appears in that text is n_a, then the probability of picking the letter 'a' is n_a/N. If we then pick a second letter in the same text, the probability of that being the letter 'a' is $(n_a -1)/(N-1)$. The probability of the first and second letters being the same is those two multiplied together. It is then possible to work out the index of coincidence (IC) for the entire alphabet by adding the probabilities for every letter together.

$$IC = c \times \left(\left(\frac{n_a}{N} \times \frac{n_a-1}{N-1} \right) + \left(\frac{n_b}{N} \times \frac{n_b-1}{N-1} \right) + \cdots + \left(\frac{z}{N} \times \frac{n_z-1}{N-1} \right) \right)$$

Note that c is a constant (typically chosen to be 26 for the number of letters in the alphabet).

We know from frequency analysis (see pages 30–35) that letters do not appear with the same frequency in a given language. If every letter appeared with the same frequency then IC would be equal to 1. However, what we find is that every language has a different value of IC, since different letters are more common in different languages. Cryptographer William F Friedman, who devised the index, found IC had the following values for the major languages:

Language	Index of coincidence
English	1.73
French	2.02
German	2.05
Italian	1.94
Portuguese	1.94
Russian	1.76
Spanish	1.94

On the face of it, knowing the index of coincidence for the language you are trying to decrypt seems little more than an interesting statistic. However, Friedman realized it had enormous potential when it came to cracking ciphers.

Imagine a simplified alphabet with just two letters – 'x' and 'y'. In this imaginary language, 'x' is the most common letter, appearing

Letter in first message	Letter in same position in second message	Probability
X	X	80% X 80% = 64%
X	Y	80% X 20% = 16%
Y	X	20% X 80% = 16%
Y	Y	20% X 20% = 4%

80 per cent of the time, with 'y' appearing 20 per cent of the time. This means that two texts in the language have the following probabilities of letters occurring.

The probability of both letters at the same position in the two messages being the same is then 64 per cent + 4 per cent = 68 per cent.

If both messages have been encrypted using the same substitution cipher (X>Y and Y>X) then we get this same probability. Yet if one message has been encrypted (the first, say) and the other not we get a different table of probabilities.

The probability of getting the same letters in the two is now just 16 percent +16 percent = 32 percent.

We can use this difference to use the index of coincidence to help break polyalphabetic ciphers. When someone has used a polyaphabetic cipher, we are unlikely to know the number of cipher alphabets that have been used. However, we can break the text into chunks of equal size (starting with two) and line them up in columns. For example, with ciphertext that starts **JPJDRSKZBASETRAXKJ** ... we could divide it up as follows:

Suspected number of cipher alphabets	2	3	4	5	6
	JP	JPJ	JPJD	JPJDR	JPJDRS
	JD	DRS	RSKZ	SKZBA	KZBASE
	RS	KZB	BASE	SETRA	TRAXKJ
	...	...	...	...	...

By calculating the index of coincidence for each column of characters, we should find that one column closely matches Friedman's value of IC for that particular language. That reveals the number of alphabets used. Once this is established, it is a question of using traditional frequency analysis to find the letter substitutions. A more detailed explanation of the system is given in Friedman's work *The Index of Coincidence and its Application in Cryptanalysis*.

JEFFERSON'S CRYPTOGRAPH

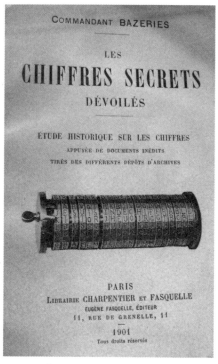

1790–1914

A simple cylinder with movable discs is believed to have been invented many times through history, including by third US president Thomas Jefferson. The system uses multiple alphabets to conceal a message.

COMMANDANT BAZERIES

LES

CHIFFRES SECRETS

DÉVOILÉS

ÉTUDE HISTORIQUE SUR LES CHIFFRES
APPUYÉE DE DOCUMENTS INÉDITS
TIRÉS DES DIFFÉRENTS DÉPÔTS D'ARCHIVES

PARIS
LIBRAIRIE CHARPENTIER ET FASQUELLE
EUGÈNE FASQUELLE, ÉDITEUR
11, RUE DE GRENELLE, 11

1901
Tous droits réservés

Étienne Bazeries' Les chiffres secrets dévoilés *contains an illustration of Bazeries cylindrical cryptograph. While Bazeries claimed the invention, the same idea was also proposed by Thomas Jefferson one hundred years earlier.*

It is often the case in the world of innovation that two or more people independently come up with the same idea. The cylindrical cryptograph is an example of this.

Between 1790 and 1793, Thomas Jefferson – later to become third president of the United States – was acting as George Washington's Secretary of State. During this time, he developed an idea for a cipher system using rotating alphabetic discs to replace each letter of a plaintext message.

More than a century later, in 1901, French cryptanalyst Étienne Bazeries published the book *Les chiffres secrets dévoilés (Secret Ciphers Revealed)*. Inside, he details an almost identical cylinder, an illustration of which is shown on the book's cover, but claims invention for himself. The Bazeries cylinder had one important improvement on Jefferson's – the order of the discs was shuffled based on a key that was shared between sender and recipient.

Fast forward 13 years and US Army Colonel Parker Hitt invented the cylinder yet again, and it became the basis for the M-94 cipher used by the US military. Colonel Hitt claimed never to have heard of Bazeries' or Jefferson's devices and Bazeries makes no mention of Jefferson in his book. Great minds clearly do think alike.

Given the large number of alphabets used (36), the cylindrical cryptograph challenges the power of frequency analysis, since the greater the number of alphabets used, the more ciphertext a codebreaker will need to use the technique effectively. Yet messages sent using the Jefferson cylinder are vulnerable to eavesdropping by an enemy who manages to obtain a cylinder, since the discs are always used in the same order.

The Bazeries version is more complex, but it also has a vulnerability in that the same offset – the number of turns of each disc between the plaintext and ciphertext letter – is used on each disc no matter what order

Former US President Thomas Jefferson's notes on his wheel cipher system, which he developed between 1790 and 1793. After a few revisions by others, this system was subsequently used by the US military.

the discs are placed on the spindle. If the codebreaker has a crib – such as a salutation of 'Dear Mr President' – at the beginning, this can be used to break the cipher. The codebreaker creates a grid showing the offset between each plaintext and corresponding ciphertext character in the message for every numbered disc. The actual offset figure is likely to be the most commonly repeated number in the table. By ignoring all other numbers in the grid, the columns can be reordered until a diagonal of this number becomes visible, revealing the order of the discs.

The M-94 cylinder, based on Colonel Hitt's idea, featured 25 aluminium discs which could be loaded in any order onto an aluminium road. Each disc featured the 26 letters of the alphabet in a scrambled order. The large number of different ways to order the discs (25 factorial or more than 15 septillion) meant that the M-94 was an exceptionally secure device for use in the field and it came into use in 1922, with the US Navy adopting its own version in 1926. However, even with this enormous number of possible keys, the cipher could still be cracked if enough ciphertext were available. Even so, the M-94 was used extensively by the US military until 1945.

Using the code

Jefferson's notes for making and using the cylinder suggest taking a cylinder of wood, 15–20 cm (6–8 in) long and 5 cm(2 in) in diameter, and boring a hole through its length. The cylinder surface is divided into 26 parts along its length and parallel lines inked in. The cylinder is cut into 36 discs, each around one-sixth of an inch wide and numbered consecutively. Each disc is then inscribed with the letters of the alphabet in a jumbled order, different for each disc. Finally, the discs are mounted on an iron spindle in numerical order.

To encrypt a message, the sender turns the discs so that the message appears in a row. The sender then writes down any one of the other 25 rows of characters and sends this message to the recipient who has an identically arranged cylinder. The recipient adjusts his cylinder to read the same and then simply examines the other 25 rows to find a message that makes sense.

MORSE CODE

The dots and dashes of the SOS message are widely known, but it wasn't always meant to be that way. The story begins with a bereavement during the first half of the nineteenth century.

Samuel Morse (1792–1872), inventor of the telegraph which revolutionized nineteenth-century communication.

Ask most people what dot-dot-dot, dash-dash-dash, dot-dot-dot means and they will quickly be able to tell you it is the radio distress signal SOS. Yet if Samuel Morse's original plan for his code was still in use, things would be very different.

Morse's interest in codes came about indirectly from his work as a portrait painter. In 1825 while working away from home, he received a letter saying his wife was ill. Unfortunately, by the time he was able to return home, she had died and been buried. Morse felt that there must be a way to speed up long distance communication.

Morse had previously studied electricity at Yale College and wondered whether it might offer a solution to the timeliness of messages. After seeing experiments with electromagnets, Morse came up with the idea of the single-wire telegraph and patented it. While most people today think of operators listening to Morse code through headsets, the original telegraph design made indentations on a tape advanced by clockwork. The receiving operator would decrypt the code to reveal the intended message.

The message that Morse sent at the 1843 official opening of the line between Washington and Baltimore. The line was 38 miles long!

Morse's young assistant Alfred Vail helped overcome some of the practical problems with the system and on 11 January, 1838, Morse and Vail gave the first demonstration of a transmission in Morse code at a house in Morristown, New Jersey. Five years later, the US Congress approved the construction of a $30,000 60-km (38-mile) telegraph line between the Capitol building in Washington and the Mount Clare Station in Baltimore, Maryland.

On 24 May 1844, the telegraph line was officially opened and Morse sent the now-famous message 'What hath God wrought' from one end of the line to Vail at the other end.

The success of Morse's demonstration led to the rapid growth of the telegraph network in the US. By 1951, there were ten different companies running lines into New York from Philadelphia, Buffalo and Boston and the US telegraph network amounted to more than 20,000 miles of wire.

During the 1850s and 1860s, there was significant consolidation between the various competing telegraph operators. In 1861, the first transcontinental line connected California with the East Coast – leading to the demise of the Pony Express – and by 1866 Western Union emerged as the dominant power.

Understanding messages written in Morse code is really quite straightforward. Since they are based on standards, anyone who knows Morse code can simply rewrite the message. However, the power of Morse code is enhanced when it is used in conjunction with other encryption methods so that the original message is already enciphered before sending and the receiver is knows the encryption method.

Using the code

Samuel Morse's original idea had been to use special codebooks or dictionaries to encrypt messages – the intention was not to hide the message, but to make it quicker to send. The sender would look up a word in the codebook and find a corresponding numerical code. This code would then be transmitted using the telegraph. The recipient would then do the reverse.

Vail realized that the system was slow and difficult to use in practise and came up with several improvements, including the sending key, and the move away from dictionaries to the American Morse Code, which was in place by the time 'What hath God wrought' was sent.

The American Morse Code used nine different lengths of dots, dashes, and spaces to encode letters, numerals, and symbols (shown in the graphic above.) A particular feature is that there are different lengths of spaces between letters of a word, between two words, and at the ends of sentences to help the receiver distinguish these groups. The code spread quickly as telegraph networks expanded across America, Latin America, and Europe.

The Morse code known today – through the SOS symbol – was largely devised by the German telegraphy pioneer Friedrich Clemens Gerke. Gerke simplified the code by reducing the number of dash durations and assigning shorter codes to the most commonly used letters. An international standard was finally adopted in 1865. Usage of Morse code dramatically increased with the advent of wireless radio telegraphy during the late nineteenth century.

PLAYFAIR CIPHER

A cipher that its creator considered simple enough for elementary children to use was adopted by the British military during both the Boer War and World War I.

Sir Charles Wheatstone (top) and Lyon Playfair (bottom). Both of these men helped to commercialize ciphers in the twentieth century.

Sir Charles Wheatstone was a British inventor and pioneer of electricity and telegraphy. Along with William Cooke, he developed the first commercial system of telegraphs.

Wheatstone also had an interest in ciphers and spent much time studying and discussing them with his London neighbour Lyon Playfair, the Scottish scientist and Liberal politician. One of their favoured pastimes was cracking ciphers that appeared regularly in personal advertisements in *The Times* newspaper. Wheatstone also invented his own cipher, which became known as the Playfair cipher, after his friend who helped promote its use.

Playfair hides the frequency of individual letters, because the same letter can become different ciphertext characters. This means that standard frequency analysis will not work. However, analysis of digraph frequency can produce results. A cipher can be identified as a Playfair by recognizing that there are no repeated double letters, since they are split with a null character and that either I or J remains unused.

Using the cipher

Dorothy L Sayers used the Playfair cipher in her 1932 Lord Peter Wimsey novel *Have His Carcase.*

'You choose a keyword of six letters or more, none of which recurs. Such as, for example, SQUANDER. *Then you make a diagram of five squares each way and write the keyword in the squares . . . Then you fill up the remaining spaces with the rest of the alphabet in order, leaving out the ones you've already got . . .*

Now let's take a message . . . "All is known, fly at once" . . . and break it into groups of two letters, reading from left to right. It won't do to have two of the same letters coming together, so where that happens we shove in q or z or something . . .

So now our message runs: al ql is kn ow nf ly at on ce.'

'Suppose there was an odd letter at the end?'

'Well then we'd add on another q or z or something to square it up.'

S	Q	U	A	N
D	E	R	B	C
F	G	H	IJ	K
L	M	O	P	T
V	W	X	Y	Z

'Now we take our first group, al. We see that they come at the corners of a rectangle in which the other corners are sp. So we put down sp for the first two letters of the coded message. In the same way ql becomes sm and is becomes fa.'

Where the two characters appear in the same column, such as AP, the two characters below them are used (BY). For characters on the same row – MP – the next characters to the right are used (OT). The ciphertext can be broken into groups of any length, with random punctuation, and the recipient simply puts the characters in pairs and reverses the operation.

Beaufort Cipher

1830–1857

A cipher created by a renowned naval officer was used to conceal family secrets in his journals and letters.

Francis Beaufort was born in Ireland in 1774 and left home at the age of 13 for a life at sea, fighting in the Napoleonic Wars. In 1806, he invented a scale based on the area of sail that crews needed to hoist at various levels of storm to be able to handle a ship's motion in the water; the Beaufort scale was adopted by the British Navy some 30 years later, ensuring his name remains known to this day.

Beaufort's cipher became known to the wider public only after his death when his son William published a 11.4 x 13cm (4½ x 5 in) stiff paper card sold for sixpence called *Cryptography, A System of Secret Writing . . . adapted for Telegrams, and Postage Cards*. In fact, the system had previously been published by Giovanni Sestri more than 150 years but its use was largely ignored and the Beaufort name remains.

The Beaufort's similarity to the Vigenère means that it is susceptible to the same decryption methods. The polymath Charles Babbage was one of Beaufort's friends and had a healthy interest in cryptanalysis and is known to have discovered the conservation law method of solving polyalphabetic ciphers like the Vigenère cipher in 1831 or perhaps even earlier.

Certainly by 1853 Babbage had shown that he was able to solve any of the group of Vigenère ciphers by solving a simultaneous set of related monoalphabetic ciphers. This method is today better known as Kasiski analysis, after Friedrich Kasiski who discovered the technique independently and published a book on it in 1863 (see page 122.)

Using the cipher

The cipher that Beaufort created is a modified version of the Vigenère cipher (see page 69). Like the Vigenère, Beaufort uses a tabula recta, which has the alphabet running along all four sides. Let us say that we

A	B	C	D	E	F	G	H	I	J	K	L	M	N	O	P	Q	R	S	T	U	V	W	X	Y	Z	A
B	C	D	E	F	G	H	I	J	K	L	M	N	O	P	Q	R	S	T	U	V	W	X	Y	Z	A	B
C	D	E	F	G	H	I	J	K	L	M	N	O	P	Q	R	S	T	U	V	W	X	Y	Z	A	B	C
D	E	F	G	H	I	J	K	L	M	N	O	P	Q	R	S	T	U	V	W	X	Y	Z	A	B	C	D
E	F	G	H	I	J	K	L	M	N	O	P	Q	R	S	T	U	V	W	X	Y	Z	A	B	C	D	E
F	G	H	I	J	K	L	M	N	O	P	Q	R	S	T	U	V	W	X	Y	Z	A	B	C	D	E	F
G	H	I	J	K	L	M	N	O	P	Q	R	S	T	U	V	W	X	Y	Z	A	B	C	D	E	F	G
H	I	J	K	L	M	N	O	P	Q	R	S	T	U	V	W	X	Y	Z	A	B	C	D	E	F	G	H
I	J	K	L	M	N	O	P	Q	R	S	T	U	V	W	X	Y	Z	A	B	C	D	E	F	G	H	I
J	K	L	M	N	O	P	Q	R	S	T	U	V	W	X	Y	Z	A	B	C	D	E	F	G	H	I	J
K	L	M	N	O	P	Q	R	S	T	U	V	W	X	Y	Z	A	B	C	D	E	F	G	H	I	J	K
L	M	N	O	P	Q	R	S	T	U	V	W	X	Y	Z	A	B	C	D	E	F	G	H	I	J	K	L
M	N	O	P	Q	R	S	T	U	V	W	X	Y	Z	A	B	C	D	E	F	G	H	I	J	K	L	M
N	O	P	Q	R	S	T	U	V	W	X	Y	Z	A	B	C	D	E	F	G	H	I	J	K	L	M	N
O	P	Q	R	S	T	U	V	W	X	Y	Z	A	B	C	D	E	F	G	H	I	J	K	L	M	N	O
P	Q	R	S	T	U	V	W	X	Y	Z	A	B	C	D	E	F	G	H	I	J	K	L	M	N	O	P
Q	R	S	T	U	V	W	X	Y	Z	A	B	C	D	E	F	G	H	I	J	K	L	M	N	O	P	Q
R	S	T	U	V	W	X	Y	Z	A	B	C	D	E	F	G	H	I	J	K	L	M	N	O	P	Q	R
S	T	U	V	W	X	Y	Z	A	B	C	D	E	F	G	H	I	J	K	L	M	N	O	P	Q	R	S
T	U	V	W	X	Y	Z	A	B	C	D	E	F	G	H	I	J	K	L	M	N	O	P	Q	R	S	T
U	V	W	X	Y	Z	A	B	C	D	E	F	G	H	I	J	K	L	M	N	O	P	Q	R	S	T	U
V	W	X	Y	Z	A	B	C	D	E	F	G	H	I	J	K	L	M	N	O	P	Q	R	S	T	U	V
W	X	Y	Z	A	B	C	D	E	F	G	H	I	J	K	L	M	N	O	P	Q	R	S	T	U	V	W
X	Y	Z	A	B	C	D	E	F	G	H	I	J	K	L	M	N	O	P	Q	R	S	T	U	V	W	X
Y	Z	A	B	C	D	E	F	G	H	I	J	K	L	M	N	O	P	Q	R	S	T	U	V	W	X	Y
Z	A	B	C	D	E	F	G	H	I	J	K	L	M	N	O	P	Q	R	S	T	U	V	W	X	Y	Z
A	B	C	D	E	F	G	H	I	J	K	L	M	N	O	P	Q	R	S	T	U	V	W	X	Y	Z	A

want to encipher the plaintext 'Meet me at the Eiffel Tower' and that the key we have chosen is 'hurricane'.

To encrypt a letter we look along either of the outer bold alphabets until we reach the first letter of the plaintext, in this case **M**. We then move our finger along the row or column until we reach the first letter of the key, **H**. At **H**, we then turn right angles and move along the column or row till we reach the outside, where we read off the outer bold letter, in our case **V**. This is the ciphertext. The full message is encrypted below.

Deciphering the message uses exactly the same technique – the Beaufort is therefore one of a class called reciprocal ciphers. This method is known as the true Beaufort to be distinguished from what is known as the variant Beaufort, in which you start by choosing the first letter of the key in the outer bold alphabet and then moving along to find the first letter of the plaintext within the table.

Plaintext	m	e	e	t	m	e	a	t	t	h	e	e	i	f	f	e	l	t	o	w	e	r
Key	H	U	R	R	I	C	A	N	E	H	U	R	R	I	C	A	N	E	H	U	R	R
Ciphertext	V	Q	N	Y	W	Y	A	U	L	A	Q	N	J	D	X	W	C	L	T	Y	N	A

CODEBREAKERS OF HISTORY

AUGUSTE KERCKHOFFS

The work of Dutch linguist Auguste Kerckhoffs underlies virtually every computer security system that we know today, although at the time he was unaware of the significance of his views.

Auguste Kerckhoffs was born in 1835 in Nuth in the Netherlands and trained at the University of Liège before becoming a teacher of modern languages and taking a position at Melun in France. In 1873, Kerckhoffs became a French citizen and, in 1878, was appointed professor of German at Paris's liberal École des Hautes Études Commerciales (HEC) and the École Arago.

He is known today for Kerckhoffs' Principle. The idea was first expounded in two journal articles published in French in *Le Journal de Sciences Militaires* in 1883 under the title 'La Cryptographie Militaire' although his reasons for doing so are unclear.

The papers describe many of the historic encryption methods described in this book, but it is the six *desiderata* he describes as prerequisites for designing a military cipher which have become associated with his name. They are translated from the French below.

1. *The system must be practically, if not mathematically, indecipherable;*
2. *It should not require secrecy, and it should not be a problem if it falls into enemy hands;*
3. *It must be possible to communicate and remember the key without using written notes, and correspondents must be able to change or modify it at will;*
4. *It must be applicable to telegraph communications;*
5. *It must be portable, and should not require several persons to handle or operate;*
6. *Lastly, given the circumstances in which it is to be used, the system must be easy to use and should not be stressful to use or require its users to know and comply with a long list of rules.*

Some of Kerckhoffs' desiderata, particularly the last three, have become obsolete or irrelevant in the modern world, particularly with the advent of computerized techniques.

The importance of indecipherability (the first axiom) even if you could change the key (the third) was explained by Kerckhoffs: 'It is enough to cite the case where the commander of a city under siege sends information to the army that must come to its aid. Moreover, once someone has managed to decipher an intercepted message, every new dispatch, encrypted with the same key and likewise intercepted, can be read instantly.'

It is the second of the axioms that has remained relevant and is known as Kerckhoffs' principle. It was later reformulated by American cryptographer Claude Shannon as 'The enemy knows the system,' which is sometimes known as 'Shannon's maxim'.

What Kerckhoffs' principle means in practice is that even if the design of a cipher machine or algorithm is known it should not endanger the security of the encryption as long as the key remains secret. An example of this is Marian Rejewski's incredible feat of working out the wiring and design of the early Enigma machines (see pages 128–129). Working for the Polish intelligence services, he applied an advanced level or pure mathematical skill to deducing out how the machines were working.

However, even with knowledge of the machine's design, the Poles still had an enormous task to decrypt messages because the key used to set the machine initially was unknown.

Virtually every encryption technique that is in use today can be shown to conform to Kerckhoffs' principle.

UNION ROUTE CIPHER

Codes played an important role in the four-year-long American Civil War between the Unionists and Confederates.

By the outbreak of the American Civil War in 1861, telegraphy was well established in the US. The network had expanded significantly since Morse's time and stretched to some 100,000 km (60,000 miles) .

In April 1861, the state governor of Ohio – one of the northern Unionist states – turned to Anson Stager, the general superintendent of the Western Union Telegraph Company, for help in communicating secretly with its allies. Stager developed what has become known as the Union Route cipher and its success led to him being appointed as head of the Military Telegraph Department later that same year. If accounts of the Civil War are to be believed, the Confederacy never broke the Union Route cipher and its use may have helped the Union to its eventual victory.

A method for cracking transposition ciphers was not invented until a decade after the Civil War. Multiple anagramming requires the use of two or more messages that have been encrypted using the same scheme.

Imagine we have a simple transposition cipher which works on six-letter words, which swaps the letters in the following manner 1st > 4th > 6th > 2nd > 5th > 3rd (> 1st). Using this, the word **STAGER** becomes **ARESTG** and **SUMTER** becomes **MRESUT**.

Say we have intercepted **ARESTG** and **MRESUT** and we make a guess that **ARESTG** is the word **GRATES** in plaintext, which would suggest the transposition method is 1st > 6th > 4th > 5th > 3rd > 1st (while 2nd stays as 2nd). If we try that in reverse on **MRESUT**, we get **TRMUES** which is not a real word so we can assume the method is incorrect and try another until we find the correct one. The same method can be employed on the Union cipher but the codewords make it far more difficult to break.

Using the cipher

The cipher Stager invented is a route cipher, where each word of the plaintext is placed in a grid and it is encrypted by rewriting the message by taking a pre-determined route around it.

The following is a telegraph message sent by Abraham Lincoln during the war.

> FOR COLONEL LUDLOW:
> RICHARDSON AND BROWN, CORRESPONDENTS OF THE
> TRIBUNE, CAPTURED AT VICKSBURG, ARE DETAINED AT
> RICHMOND. PLEASE ASCERTAIN WHY THEY ARE DETAINED
> AND GET THEM OFF IF YOU CAN.
> THE PRESIDENT.

We have placed this message in a 7x5 grid and added the null words FLOWER, HARPOON and CLOWN – words that would never normally be used in a message – to complete it.

FOR	COLONEL	LUDLOW	RICHARD-SON	AND	BROWN	CORRESPON-DENTS
OF	THE	TRIBUNE	CAPTURED	AT	VICKSBURG	AND
DETAINED	AT	RICHMOND	PLEASE	ASCERTAIN	WHY	THEY
ARE	DETAINED	AND	GET	THEM	OFF	IF
YOU	CAN	THE	PRESIDENT	FLOWER	HARPOON	CLOWN

We agree a route around the grid with the recipient – say up the first column, down the second, up the third and so on – and rewrite the message in this way to get YOU ARE DETAINED OF FOR COLONEL THE AT DETAINED CAN THE AND RICHMOND TRIBUNE . . .

One improvement to reduce decipherability was to replace certain common words and phrases with codewords. Some of the replacements used include VENUS for COLONEL, NEPTUNE for RICHMOND, for example. Some terms, such as President Lincoln, had multiple codewords, including ADAM and BOLOGNA.

CODEBREAKERS OF HISTORY

ELIZEBETH FRIEDMAN

Elizebeth Friedman, née Smith, was born in 1892 and majored in English but had also studied other languages including German and Latin. At the age of 24, Elizebeth was working at Chicago's Newberry Library when she was recruited by a wealthy textile merchant, George Fabyan, who had established a so-called 'Department of Ciphers' alongside private laboratories studying chemistry and genetics at his Illinois estate Riverbank. There she would assist with an attempt to identify and decrypt hidden messages in the works of Shakespeare.

At Riverbank, Elizebeth met William F Friedman, head of Fabyan's genetics lab, and they married in 1917. As America entered the war against Germany, Fabyan offered Riverbank's services to the government. Elizebeth dropped her Shakespeare work and William his genetics and together they became involved in decrypting German messages.

After the war, the Friedmans were taken on by the government. William was hired by the War Department as chief cryptanalyst while Elizebeth started as an assistant.

Elizebeth later worked for the US Navy before being transferred to work with the US Treasury Bureau of Prohibition and the Coast Guard. This involved her in working against criminal syndicates. The 'rumrunners' of the time were using coded radio messages and in her first three years in the job she decrypted more than 12,000 of these.

In 1937, she was asked by the Canadian government to help smash an opium smuggling ring. Without knowledge of the Chinese language used, she managed to crack the code of the smugglers and the gang were imprisoned for seven years on her evidence.

Elizebeth's involvement was crucial in the Doll Woman Case. From 1937, Velvalee Dickinson and her husband Lee ran an antique doll shop in Madison Avenue, New York, which catered to wealthy collectors. Shortly after the Japanese attacks on Pearl Harbor, the FBI intercepted a letter supposedly sent by a woman in Portland, Oregon to a contact in Buenos

Aires, Argentina. It was picked out by wartime censors because of the unusual language. The FBI also intercepted four other letters, all related to dolls, which were sent to the same individual in Argentina but failed to reach their destination. When the FBI spoke with the senders, they denied any knowledge of them.

One of the letters included the sentence 'you wrote to me that you had sent a letter to Mr Shaw, well I went to see MR SHAW he destroyed (sic) YOUR letter, you know he has been ill. His car was damaged but is being repaired now.' According to FBI archives, Friedman recognized that the letter was actually referring to the US Navy destroyer *Shaw*, which had been damaged at Pearl Harbor and had been repaired and was being returned to active service.

Other letters contained similar information about US Navy ships, their location and state of repair – information of vital importance to the Japanese. Experts showed that all of the letters had been composed on the same typewriter and it came to light that all of the supposed senders had done business with Dickinson. When she was investigated, the FBI discovered she had a huge number of $100 banknotes, some of which could be traced as having been given to high-ranking Japanese officials before the start of the war.

If Dickinson had been found guilty of espionage she could have faced the death penalty. Instead, when the case came to court in 1944, Dickinson was permitted to plead guilty to the lesser charge of censorship violation and admitted that she had written the letters and that details of the code had been given to her and her husband in late 1941 by Japanese Naval Attaché Ichiro Yokoyama. She was sentenced to ten years in prison.

COMMERCIAL CODES

The prohibitive cost of sending telegraphic messages in the early days led to the codebooks that sought to reduce the cost by condensing phrases into single words or numerical codes.

The cover of a commercial codebook telling the reader how to communicate without using full words. The book helped keep costs down, as telegraphs charged per word in the 1880s.

In 1884, Western Union was charging 50 cents (the equivalent of approximately $13 today) per word to send a message by telegraph. James D Reid, in his 1886 book *The Telegraph in America and Morse Memorial*, reported that the cost of sending just ten words on the first successful transatlantic cable between New York and London was $100 ($2,700 today). Costs fell quickly, but it was still 40 cents per word just over 20 years later. Such high costs meant that those sending messages made them as short as possible while still retaining their meaning.

This financial imperative led to the development of commercial codes – books that contained lists of words that could stand in place of complete phrases. The first codebooks appeared just a few years after the commercialization of the wire telegraph, and hundreds appeared over the next few decades.

As well as codes for general correspondence, some industries developed their own codebooks, which contained abbreviated ways to send specialized vocabulary. Examples include Clough's 1896 mining code, Farquhar's 1909 system for bankers, brokers, and investors, and Fallon's 1922 code for use in the California tinned fruit industry.

Cracking the code

Commercial codes were mainly designed to save money for those sending messages. However, some served the dual purpose of hiding the content of the message – useful if the content of the message was private or contained commercial secrets.

Using the code

Francis John Bolton's 1868 patent code replaced short phrases with four-digit numbers that were more economical to send. It was divided into commercial phrases and more general correspondence. The code **1029** meant 'Advise us of state of market' while **0217** meant 'Come as quickly as you can'.

The Unicode system used previously agreed Latin words to replace phrases and was designed to avoid regular misunderstandings that accompanied telegraphic messaging. The system coded the message 'Confined to-day. Baby dead. Mother very weak', a relatively common message for a doctor at the time, using the word AMYLON and the message 'Confined to-day. Twins, both boys, all well' as ANCILIUM. There is no method to recreate these code words from the original message but since sender and recipient both have copies of the codebooks, understanding what the messages said was easy.

Clough's mining code broke down commonly used phrases into different groups, one set for mining company names, another for terms used in the industry. Anglo-American became the word 'acquaint' while the term 'pelecoid' stood for 'Where is the company's headquarters located?,' meaning six words could be replaced with just one.

David Kahn, in his classic book *The Codebreakers*, tells of the Primrose v Western Union Telephone Company case in the Supreme Court, which relates to commercial codes. A wool dealer argued that an error by a telegrapher cost $20,000 due to misread instructions. The Supreme Court ruled that the telegraphy company was liable only for the $1.15 cost of the message.

A page from Bolton's Patent Code for Transmitting Messages by Electric or Magnetic Telegraph from 1868. Short and generic phrases were replaced by four digits in order to make messaging quick and economical.

Q and Z Codes

Communication between ships was difficult, even with the advent of radio telegraphy, and this led to the development of coding methods that were even shorter to transmit than standard Morse code.

Morse code dominated communication during the nineteenth and early twentieth centuries, yet some users needed an even more succinct way of transmitting messages. The British authorities introduced a series of codes that were used for brevity, known as Q codes. Here, frequently used messages were shortened to three-letter codes beginning with 'q'. They were then translated into Morse code, saving both time and money.

The brevity of Q codes was particularly advantageous for shipping and, later, aviation, both of which were prone to weak signals. By the 1970s, there were more than one hundred different Q codes in use. As the use of Morse code declined with the rise of voice communications, Q codes eventually disappeared from most areas.

Z codes, employed by NATO, use Z for the initial character. The Combined Communications Electronics Board's document ACP 131(F) includes a comprehensive list of both Q and Z codes, including ZGG – 'What is the call sign of the friendly striking force aircraft?'

Cracking the code

Q codes are standardized by design, meaning that anyone can interpret them. As with Morse code, they can be encrypted using another scheme before sending. With standardized messages like these, the underlying scheme can sometimes be guessed at. For example, if a warship always began its messages with QRA (see opposite), an eavesdropper could use that as a crib to then recognize which characters represented the encrypted name of the ship. If the eavesdropper knew the general movements of an enemy fleet, then the ship's name could be guessed and the encryption method revealed.

Using the code

The 1909 *Handbook for Wireless Telegraph Operators* by His Majesty's Postmaster-General in Britain was the first to outline the use of Q codes. This was then standardized in 1912 as follows:

The same code could be used as a question or answer, depending on whether it was followed by a question mark (·· − −·· in Morse). The Q code would be repeated three times and the answer (indicated by a blank) would follow.

An interchange between a costal station and a ship might have gone as follows:

QRA QRA QRA ·· − − ··

QRA QRA QRA TITANIC

(Note that QRA would be signaled in Morse as − −·− ·−· ·−)

This code would mean:

'Which ship or coast station is that?'

'This is Titanic.'

The saving in time and resource is clear: these messages in Q code would be transmitted with far fewer characters than the full-text messages they represent. The aviation sector still uses Q codes. The International Civil Aviation Organization's list of standardized codes and abbreviations includes QFE for determining the atmospheric pressure at an aerodrome, QGE for establishing the distance to a station, and QDR for establishing the magnetic bearing. These days, the codes are transmitted, not by Morse code, but by voice and, sometimes in aviation, by automated message.

CODEBREAKERS OF HISTORY

AGNES MEYER DRISCOLL (MADAME X)

Born Agnes May Meyer in Geneseo, Illinois in 1889, Agnes Meyer Driscoll was an important figure in the development of cryptography in the US. She is best remembered as Madame X, a nickname that was bestowed on her by her male colleagues in her work as a cryptanalyst.

Agnes Meyer Driscoll earned the nickname 'Madame X' due to her notoriety as a cryptanalyst among male colleagues.

Prior to 1918, the United States had little in the way of defensive ciphers and codes. That had to change and Driscoll's role proved to be crucial yet her work with the military only came about because of a legal loophole.

The German sinking of US naval vessels and the entry of the country into World War I in 1917 found the navy significantly understaffed. Yet the vague language of the Naval Act of a year earlier, which called for 'persons who may be capable of performing special useful service for coastal defence', had an unexpected result – it meant that women were allowed to enlist for the first time, albeit in administrative roles.

Driscoll was one of those who answered the navy's call and on 22 June 1918, she enlisted. Her first role was in the Postal and Cable Censorship Office where she reviewed correspondence for evidence of espionage, but within a year she was moved to the Code and Signal Section (CSS). And in 1919 and 1920 Driscoll is thought to have spent several months in Herbert O Yardley's Cipher Bureau, the so-called American Black Chamber.

In 1921, in conjunction with the head of the section, Lieutenant Commander William Gresham, Driscoll designed a mechanical cipher device called the Cipher Machine or CM Driscoll came up with the encipherment method and Gresham worked out the mechanical details. The machine contained several printed paper alphabets that were moved by a stylus in which the movement of one strip also moved the other alphabets along a step. She left the service briefly in 1923 to help Edward Hebern in his work with one of the first rotor machines (see page 124), but an evaluation by William F Friedman showed that it had shortcomings and she returned to the Code and Signal Section in 1924.

Agnes was assigned to the Research Desk, which was engaged in cryptanalysis, the interception and breaking of the codes and ciphers used in Japanese communications. The first code that Driscoll helped to break was known as the Red Book. Naval spies had managed to break into the Japanese Consul General's safe and photographed each page of a codebook. The copies were held in a red folder, hence the name.

In 1926, Driscoll managed to break the first key and message traffic was readable for several weeks. More complicated keys were subsequently used, but Driscoll and the Research Desk remained on top of them.

After four years of reading Japanese traffic, the method of encryption suddenly changed, but Driscoll was up to the challenge. Unlike the previous case where they had a stolen codebook to work from, this time they had to recreate the book themselves – this new code was stored in a blue folder and became known as the Blue Book code.

It helped that the Japanese used a superencipherment transposition method so Driscoll was able to use this to unravel the code numbers – of which there were 85,000 – but even so it took Driscoll and her team three years to work out the Blue Book Code. A key discovery made from the messages was that the then new Japanese Kongo class battlecruiser had a top speed of 26 knots; the US North Carolina Class battleships were modified to have higher top speeds as a result.

Driscoll continued her work into the 1930s and into the World War II, but it is her prodigious efforts in cracking the Japanese naval codes that proved to be her zenith. Her work on them was one of the last great manual decryption endeavours; the rise of the machine age meant that such methods would soon be consigned to history.

ADFGX and ADFGVX Ciphers

Two ciphers used by the German army were cracked by a
French army officer with an amateur interest in cryptology
and cryptanalysis.

Georges-Jean Painvin, born in 1886, was a graduate of the 'X', France's famous
École Polytechnique, and left to become an engineer in the Corps des mines.
During World War I, he was a captain in the French 6th Army, based in
Villers-Cotterets. In January 1915, Painvin sent a message to the Cabinet Noir,
the body that intercepted suspect letters, explaining an ingenious system for
cracking any message encrypted with the ABC cipher, used by the German
military, even if only one ciphertext had been intercepted.

The quality of work was recognized by the Minister of War Alexandre
Millerand, who suggested Painvin come and work in the Cabinet Noir.
An initial two-week trial period turned into a four-year stint in France's
cryptography service.

Painvin's biggest achievement was in the decryption of the ADFGX and the
more complicated ADFGVX cipher introduced by the German high command
in March 1918.

Painvin's breakthrough with the ADFGX cipher came when he realized that
the key changed each day and that to stand a chance of breaking it he needed
many messages from the same day. He guessed that many messages would
start with similar words and that these would be fractionated in a similar way
(fractionation is a cipher method that converts individual plaintext symbols
into several ciphertext symbols – see glossary page 166).

Even knowing this, decryption was manual and hugely time-consuming.
On 1 June 1918, the Cabinet Noir intercepted what became known as the
Radiogramme de la victoire, or Victory Telegram. What surprised Painvin was
the sudden appearance of the letter 'V'.

This increased the original grid from 25 squares to 36. Painvin had luck on
his side, guessing that the additional spaces were to replace the numbers 0 to 9
and to allow I and J to have their own spaces.

After receiving the 1 June telegram, he worked without stopping for 26
hours and, once the decryption was complete, collapsed into his bed. The

exhaustion caused by his work on the ADFGX and ADFGVX ciphers led to him being hospitalized and then being forced to convalesce for several months. Meanwhile, the decryption of telegrams in ADFGVX helped thwart the German Spring Offensive.

Using the code

The first step is to draw up a Polybius square (see page 25) but using the letters **ADFGX** instead of numbers, as follows.

	A	D	F	C	X
A	A	B	C	D	E
D	F	G	H	I/J	K
F	L	M	N	O	P
C	Q	R	S	T	U
X	V	W	X	Y	Z

Note that the choice of the letters a, d, f, g, v and x is not random. The cipher was used to encrypt Morse code and dot-dash combinations of these are hard for telegraph operators to confuse; a is ·–, d is –··, f is ··–·, g is – –· and x is –··–.

Say we wish to encrypt the message 'The Germans are coming', this would be encrypted (folllowing the Polybius method) as

GGDFAX DDAXGDFDAAFFGF AAGDAX AFFGFDDGFFDD

Next, we choose a key word. **FRANCE**. We place these letters across the top of a grid as shown above and place the letters of the encrypted message beneath. We then rearrange the grid so that the letters of the key word are in alphabetical order and then read off the letters down each column (excluding the letters of the key) to produce the ciphertext.

DAAAAD AGFGFF XDFDGF GDFGAFD FXAAFG GDDFXDD

The challenge for the would-be codebreaker is clear – plaintext characters are enciphered as digrams and those are then split and transposed, or fractionated.

Tableau de Concordance

The use of cryptography on the battlefield is a challenge and this was particularly evident in World War I. As we have seen elsewhere in this book, there existed a number of secure techniques for encrypting telegraphic and radio signals, but these were often no good in the heat of battle.

One of the major problems is getting code books out to soldiers in the field and replacing them regularly if a book falls into enemy hands. The result is that many nations developed field or trench codes and ciphers which, while being less secure than other available methods, were good enough to be used on the battlefield.

One of the frequently used techniques to create a field code is called super-encipherment and involves using two steps. During World War I, the French used what was known as a *tableau de concordance* (a cross-reference table) to add a layer of security to a simple codebook system.

Using the code

The code is a two-part code, involving two steps of encryption.

The first step uses a simple commercial codebook (see pages 104–105) where each word or expression is represented by a four digit number; some 2300 words and phrases were encoded in this way. For example *soixante* (sixty) is represented by 9518, terrain by the number 3739 and the question *Avez-vous besoin de* (do you need...?) by 0784.

For regularly used words, there were several available numeric codes. For example, *trois* (three) could be encoded as 9358, 2599 or 1050. Frequently used words could also be broken down into smaller elements. For example the word *patrouille* (patrol) could be encoded as follows:

PA	TR	OU	ILLE
4620	7663	8817	0773

The instructions for using the code expressly stated that the whole message must be encoded and if there was not enough time to encrypt a message entirely, it should be transmitted as plaintext so as to avoid giving codebreakers a partially coded message, which would make their task easier.

The second step of the code is what makes the French code much harder to crack and uses the tableau de concordance, an example of which is shown below.

Say we have encoded the following message:

La	Relève	au-	ra	Lieu	demain matin
1651	4275	0865	8750	1065	7353

We then divide these numbers up into groups of two but starting and ending with a single digit and replacing the resulting two digit codes with the corresponding letter pairs in the *chiffrement* section of the *tableau de concordance*.

This method of encryption ensured that the same numeric code was not superenciphered in the same way each time. The recipient would take the ciphertext and arrange it into groups of two letters and then use the *déchiffrement* table (right) to yield the code numbers.

One of the challenges in the field is what happens if a copy falls into enemy hands. In his book *The Codebreakers*, David Kahn states that the French changed their code system three times between 1 August 1914 and 15 January 1915, for example. William F Friedman's useful overview of field codes in World War I shows that the French used at least 65 different tableaux.

CHIFFREMENT.

0 – GS	30 – HR	70 – AN
1 – RH	31 – IA	71 – RB
2 – AM	32 – VS	72 – HN
3 – SI	33 – GU	73 – MH
4 – BH	34 – NH	74 – GD
5 – NS	35 – IS	75 – BU
6 – DA	36 – HD	76 – IE
7 – TD	37 – TA	77 – DM
8 – EA	38 – IB	78 – AI
9 – UG	39 – AE	79 – RN
00 – AT	40 – HT	80 – UH
01 – GA	41 – SD	81 – NR
02 – IM	42 – US	82 – AD
03 – DN	43 – DI	83 – BM
04 – GH	44 – EI	84 – GI
05 – MN	45 – BS	85 – ED
06 – HI	46 – GR	86 – HB
07 – VG	47 – MD	87 – NA
08 – UR	48 – IR	88 – ER
09 – AB	49 – EM	89 – BG
10 – BT	50 – AU	90 – SN
11 – BA	51 – SM	91 – AS
12 – RD	52 – DB	92 – MS
13 – ND	53 – RS	93 – BD
14 – AG	54 – GB	94 – IN
15 – TS	55 – UA	95 – DS
16 – EU	56 – DA	96 – HM
17 – AR	57 – BI	97 – EH
18 – SB	58 – TR	98 – GT
19 – BN	59 – EB	99 – GN
20 – ES	60 – AH	
21 – RT	61 – VN	
22 – HA	62 – TN	
23 – DG	63 – BG	
24 – SR	64 – MU	
25 – BE	65 – NR	
26 – DT	66 – NG	
27 – NU	67 – SH	
28 – GM	68 – UM	
29 – NB	69 – DH	

DÉCHIFFREMENT.

AB – 09	EM – 49	ND – 13
AD – 82	ER – 88	NG – 66
AE – 39	ES – 20	NH – 34
AG – 14		NR – 81
AH – 60	GA – 01	NS – 5
AI – 78	GB – 54	NU – 27
AM – 2	GD – 74	
AN – 70	GH – 04	RB – 71
AR – 17	GI – 84	RD – 12
AS – 91	GM – 28	RH – 1
AT – 00	GN – 99	RN – 79
AU – 50	GR – 46	RT – 21
	GS – 0	
BA – 11	GT – 98	SB – 18
BD – 93	GU – 33	SD – 41
BE – 25		SH – 67
BG – 63	HA – 22	SI – 3
BH – 4	HB – 86	SM – 51
BI – 57	HD – 36	SN – 90
BM – 83	HI – 06	SR – 24
BN – 19	HI – 06	
BR – 65	HM – 96	TA – 37
BS – 45	HN – 72	TD – 7
BT – 10	HR – 30	TN – 62
BU – 75	HS – 63	TR – 58
	HT – 40	TS – 15
DA – 6		
DB – 52	IA – 31	UA – 55
DG – 25	IB – 38	UG – 9
DH – 69	IE – 76	UH – 80
DI – 43	IM – 02	UM – 68
DM – 77	IN – 94	UR – 08
DN – 03	IR – 48	US – 42
DR – 56	IS – 35	
DS – 95		VG – 07
DT – 26	MD – 47	VN – 61
	MH – 73	VS – 32
EA – 8	MN – 05	
EB – 59	MS – 92	
ED – 85	MU – 64	
EG – 16		
EH – 97	NA – 87	
EI – 44	NB – 29	

ZIMMERMANN TELEGRAM

It was the decryption of a German communication by Britain's Room 40 codebreaking experts that forced the United States to enter World War I, which is believed to have shortened the conflict.

By 1916, World War I was raging across Europe and two of its bloodiest battles – at the Somme and Verdun – were causing immense loss of life in the British, German and French armies. Meanwhile, on the other side of the Atlantic, the United States remained resolutely neutral. That same year, US President Woodrow Wilson was re-elected for a second term, buoyed by popular support for his stance and the political slogan, 'He kept us out of war'. That all changed in 1917. On 16 January, German Minister Arthur Zimmermann sent a telegram to the German ambassador to Mexico, Heinrich von Eckardt. The contents of the encrypted telegram fell into the hands of British cryptanalysts, who recognized an opportunity to change the course of the war.

Unbeknown to the Germans, the content of the Zimmermann telegram was intercepted by the British codebreaking team, Room 40, named after a room number in the Admiralty building in London's Whitehall. The team formed just after the start of World War I and remained at the heart of British codebreaking efforts until it was superseded by the Government Code and Cypher School in 1919, a merger of the cryptology units of the Admiralty and the War Office. This group went on to form the core of the team that was based at Bletchley Park during World War II.

The telegram had been encrypted using a code known as **0075** in which words were replaced by numbers using a codebook. Room 40 deciphered the telegram as follows:

'We intend to begin on 1 February unrestricted submarine warfare. We shall endeavour in spite of this to keep the United States of America neutral. In the event of this not succeeding, we make Mexico a proposal of alliance on the following basis: make war together, make peace together, generous financial

support, and an understanding on our part that Mexico is to reconquer the lost territory in Texas, New Mexico, and Arizona. The settlement in detail is left to you. You will inform the president of the above most secretly as soon as the outbreak of war with the United States of America is certain and add the suggestion that he should, on his own initiative, invite Japan to immediate adherence and at the same time mediate between Japan and ourselves. Please call the president's attention to the fact that the ruthless employment of our submarines now offers the prospect of compelling England in a few months to make peace.'

The Zimmermann telegram sent to the German ambassador to Mexico, Heinrich von Eckhardt. The deciphered contents fell into the hands of the US government, compelling the US to declare war.

Having deciphered the Zimmermann telegram, British intelligence faced a dilemma. They knew the telegram was political dynamite. But, at the same time, its publication would indicate to the Germans that their cipher had been broken. Then the problem was taken from their hands. A British agent in Mexico uncovered another copy of the telegram in a public telegraph office, which had been encrypted using an earlier German cipher. The telegram's contents were passed on to the US government and the message was published in American newspapers on 1 March, 1917. Congress declared war on Germany and its allies just over a month later, helping to bring the war to a speedier conclusion than would otherwise have been the case.

ONE-TIME PADS

Many seemingly unbreakable ciphers and codes have been shown to be vulnerable over time to new methods of attack. One-time pads are an important exception.

The concept of the one-time pad was first outlined in a commercial codebook called *Telegraphic Code to Insure Privacy and Secrecy in the Transmission of Telegrams*, by Frank Miller in 1882. The book improves the traditional commercial code with a method called shifted cipher.

If used correctly, the one-time pad is impossible to crack. This was eventually proven by American mathematician Claude Shannon, in a landmark 1949 paper.

He showed that if a number of conditions were met, the one-time pad is truly unbreakable. The conditions are that the key must be: truly random; at least as long as the message; kept secret; and never to be reused.

Computer scientist and mathematician Claude Shannon, pictured in 1951.

These conditions mean that, for any piece of ciphertext of a given length, it is equally likely to represent all pieces of plaintext of the same length. So ciphertext TGYHU is equally likely to represent Paris, Boise or Omaha or any other five-letter word. The problem in the real world is that these conditions are very difficult to meet and other encryption systems are more practical.

Using the code

Miller describes his shifted cipher as follows:

'A banker in the West should prepare a list of numbers to be called "shift-numbers", such as 463, 281, 175, 892, etc. The differences between such numbers must not be regular. When a shift-number has been applied, or used, it must be erased from the list and not used again.'

To encrypt a message, the banker looks at the first word or phrase of the plaintext and looks at Miller's codebook to find the matching code number for that word. The word 'Bishop', for example, has the code number 1933 in Miller's book. To this number he adds the first of the shift-numbers, making a new total. In our example, we add 463 to 1933 to get 2396. The banker then looks up the word corresponding to that new total in Miller's codebook; this word becomes the first word of the ciphertext. In our case, 2396 is the code for the word 'celerity' which we would use in our coded message. The recipient with his identical copy of the shift-number list does the same in reverse. Sadly, Miller's method was essentially forgotten.

In 1917, Gilbert Vernam, an engineer working at AT&T Bell Labs, was developing an automated cipher method for a teleprinter. His design used a similar shift to Miller's, but with binary representations of letters and a mathematical operation called an XOR, or exclusive-or (see pages 150–151). As an example the letter 'e' is represented by the code **00010**. If we wish to combine this with a key character of **11011** using the XOR rules, one digit at a time, we get:

    00010 (input 1—plaintext)
    11011 (input 2—key)
    11001 (output—ciphertext)

This output is the letter 'r', so our plaintext letter 'e' has now become **R** in ciphertext.

In the 1920s, a group of German cryptologists created one-time pads, similar to Miller's, containing sheets of random codes that could be added to numeric codes found on commercial codebooks.

CODEBREAKERS OF HISTORY

CHOCTAW AND NAVAJO CODE TALKERS

During the two World Wars, the American military used speakers of native languages to hide messages. This started when the US Army's 36th division fought on the Western Front in France in World War I, and used telephones to transmit messages but found that the Germans were eavesdropping.

A memo from Colonel A W Bloor of the 142nd Regiment to his divisional commander shows how they overcame the problem:

> *'It was remembered that the regiment possessed a company of Indians. They spoke twenty-six different languages or dialects, only four or five of which were ever written. There was hardly one chance in a million that Fritz [Germany] would be able to translate these dialects and the plan to have these Indians transmit telephone messages was adopted.'*

Fast forward to World War II and the Pacific arena. Cipher machines were now readily available, but fast-changing situations meant they were too slow for use in the field.

In 1942, World War I veteran Philip Johnston, an engineer living in California, had heard about the Choctaw code talkers and suggested a similar idea to Major J E Jones, force communication officer at Camp Elliot. Johnston was the son of a missionary and had lived among the Navajo people from the age of four, meaning he could speak the language fluently.

Speakers of native languages were utilized during the world wars by the American military. Here are Navajo code talkers serving in Bougainville, Papua New Guinea in 1943.

A demonstration to Jones showed that two Navajo men could encode, transmit and decode a three-line message in just twenty seconds. One interesting feature of both systems is that the languages do not include all the necessary military terms required to transmit messages. The Choctaw code talkers therefore used the term 'big gun' for artillery and 'little gun shoot fast' for machine gun.

The Navajo scheme was much more widely used. More than 400 Navajo speakers were recruited and a lexicon of military and more than 500 geographical terms created – 'da-he-tih-hi', which means hummingbird, for fighter plane, 'gini' or chicken hawk, for dive bomber, and 'rolled hat' for Australia. The Navajo served in every major Marine mission conducted between 1942 and 1945 in territories including Guam, Iwo Jima and Saipan.

At Iwo Jima, Major Howard Connor, 5th Marine Division signal officer, had six Navajo Code Talkers working around the clock during the first two days of the battle. Those six sent and received more than 800 messages, all without error. Major Connor declared, 'Were it not for the Navajos, the Marines would never have taken Iwo Jima'.

Both the Choctaw and Navajo codes proved impossible to crack. The renowned Navy Intelligence unit were given transmission recordings to try to decode, to check the system's strength, but gave up trying to break the Navajo code saying the language was a 'weird succession of guttural, nasal, tongue-twisting sounds'.

After the war, Japan's chief of intelligence admitted they had broken the US Air Force code but had failed miserably with the Navajo code.

Until 1968, the Navajo code talkers and their work remained secret in the interests of US national security. Finally, in 1982, the government honored them by naming 14 August 'National Navajo Code Talkers Day'.

In 2013, both the Choctaw and Navajo nations and descendants of the code talkers were awarded Congressional Gold Medals for their work.

$$y_1 = a_{21}x_1 + a_{12}x_2 + \cdots + a_{1n}x_n,$$

A	11 z	19 x	49 u	27 s	59 p	61	19	42	10	17	A
B	26 y	29 w	50 t	08 p	07 z	08	24	63	14	62	B

$$y_2 = a_{21}x_1 + a_{22}x_2 + \cdots + a_{2n}x_n,$$

C	05 x	10 t	39 s	56 z	22 y	04	26	12	52	65	C
D	36 u	09 s	13 z	12 x	17 w	32	30	11	17	06	D

$$y_2 = a_{21}x_1 + a_{22}x_2 + \cdots + a_{2n}x_n,$$

E	09 s	17 z	25 x	13 u	15 t	47	45	41	34	11	E
F	47 p	14 y	38 w	14 t	03 s	12	19	03	15	66	F

$$y_2 = a_{21}x_1 + a_{22}x_2 + \cdots + a_{2n}x_n,$$

G	12 w	16 t	56 p	09 y	42 u	30	27	02	58	57	G
H	08 t	32 p	17 y	23 w	46 x	65	09	44	02	64	H

$$y_2 = a_{21}x_1 + a_{22}x_2 + \cdots + a_{2n}x_n,$$

i	42 p	19 s	27 t	13 u	58 w	08	67	40	52	20	i
K	34 x	28 y	26 z	21 p	10 s	11	45	61	57	50	K

$$y_2 = a_{21}x_1 + a_{22}x_2 + \cdots + a_{2n}x_n,$$

L	29 t	20 u	43 w	32 x	52 y	23	09	60	49	11	L
M	27 z	27 p	33 s	41 t	15 u	52	11	09	12	59	M

$$y_2 = a_{21}x_1 + a_{22}x_2 + \cdots + a_{2n}x_n,$$

N	28 w	09 x	34 y	59 z	47 p	40	53	66	39	24	N
O	45 s	23 t	14 u	44 w	19 x	48	57	67	32	48	O

$$y_1 = a_{21}x_1 + a_{12}x_2 + \cdots + a_{1n}x_n,$$

A	11 z	19 x	49 u	27 s	59 p	61	19	42	10	17	A
B	26 y	29 w	50 t	08 p	07 z	08	24	63	14	62	B

$$y_2 = a_{21}x_1 + a_{22}x_2 + \cdots + a_{2n}x_n,$$

C	05 x	10 t	39 s	56 z	22 y	04	26	12	52	65	C
D	36 u	09 s	13 z	12 x	17 w	32	30	11	17	06	D

$$y_2 = a_{21}x_1 + a_{22}x_2 + \cdots + a_{2n}x_n,$$

E	09 s	17 z	25 x	13 u	15 t	47	45	41	34	11	E
F	47 p	14 y	38 w	14 t	03 s	12	19	03	15	66	F

$$y_2 = a_{21}x_1 + a_{22}x_2 + \cdots + a_{2n}x_n,$$

G

H

5 THE MECHANICAL ERA

y_2

i

k

y_2

L	29 t	20 u	43 w	32 x	52 y	23	09	60	49	11	L
M	27 z	27 p	33 s	41 t	15 u	52	11	09	12	59	M

$$y_2 = a_{21}x_1 + a_{22}x_2 + \cdots + a_{2n}x_n,$$

N	28 w	09 x	34 y	59 z	47 p	40	53	66	39	24	N
O	45 s	23 t	14 u	44 w	19 x	48	57	67	32	48	O

THE RISE OF THE MACHINES

At the beginning of the twentieth century, the machine was in the ascendant. It had revolutionized manufacturing, transport and communication. Until World War I, governments had seen little need for official cryptography units, but the need to keep communications secret between battlefields and military brass, particularly in global conflicts, changed all that.

The huge volume of messages meant that traditional, manual methods of encryption were no longer able to cope. Advances in mathematics also meant that encryption methods had to become more complex. Machines were perfectly suited to the task.

In the US, Edmund Hebern was one of the first to mechanize the process of encryption. His machine was shown to be insecure by chief codebreaker William F Friedman, but it kickstarted the development of machine methods. The best-known of the machines, Enigma, which came into use just as World War I ended, was invented for encrypting commercial messages but made more sophisticated for military purposes in the mid 1920s.

Machines like Enigma, Lorenz and William F Friedman's SIGABA used mechanical and electrical complexity to hide messages with a level of concealment that would have astonished earlier codebreakers.

As machines came to the fore, the field of cryptanalysis was dominated by mathematical experts rather than by amateur codebreakers. Brilliant mathematicians such as Marian Rejewski and Alan Turing used advanced techniques such as group theory, combined with practical insights, to tease out new methods to break codes. Similar techniques were used by academics at Britain's ultra-secret Bletchley Park codebreaking headquarters, but even their brilliant work would soon be eclipsed.

The Kasiski Method

One of the best known methods of cracking a polyalphabetic cipher is known as the Kasiski method, after its discoverer Freidrich Kasiski, who published it in 1863.

$$y_1 = a_{11}x_1 + a_{12}x_2 + \cdots + a_{1n}x_n,$$

At its heart, the method works by finding out the number of alphabets used. This is achieved by looking for repeated strings of characters. Consider a piece of ciphertext for 'the bigger they come the harder they fall' that reads: UJHCKJHGUUJHZERNGWIGKBTGFTWIGBGCOM.

Analysis of the text reveals a repetition of the string UJH at position 1 and position 10 and a repetition of the string WIG at positions 17 and 26. The Kasiski method assumes that identical strings are the same word encrypted by the same alphabet and that, therefore, the number of alphabets is either the difference in number of positions or some factor of that difference. Calculate this for every repetition, and the common factor of these differences is likely to be the number of alphabets used, which we call 'n'.

The ciphertext can then be divided into n smaller subsets by writing out every nth character. For example, one subset with 1st, (1+n)th, (1+2n)th, (1+3n)th letters etc, another subset with 2nd, (2+n)th, (2+2n)th, (2+3n)th letters, and so on. Each subset is then subjected to frequency analysis (see pages 30–35) as normal, since each subset has been encrypted with only one alphabet and can be tackled in the same way as a monoalphabetic cipher.

In the example above, the number of alphabets used could be nine (10–1 or 26–17) or three (since a cipher using three alphabets would repeat every nine characters.) Assuming n is three, there would be three subsets: one with 1st, 4th, 7th, 10th, etc, letters; one with 2nd, 5th, 8th, 11th, etc, letters; and one with 3rd, 6th, 9th, 12th, etc, letters.

Now they are ready for frequency analysis. Looking at the second subset, the ciphertext letter G occurs four times, so is likely to be the most common letter in English, the letter 'e', in the plaintext. Knowing this, it follows that the ciphertext string WIG represents the plaintext word 'the'. With similar educated guesses, deciphering might reveal the plaintext as: 'the bigger they come the harder they fall'. Clearly, longer ciphertexts are really needed to make best use of the Kasiski method, so that each subset is representative of the alphabet.

TypeX and SIGABA

These two cipher machines exemplify the ongoing transtion from manual to mechanical methods of encryption.

In the 1930s, US chief cryptanalyst William F Friedman designed a series of cipher machines based on the work of Auguste Kerckhoffs (see pages 98–99). The Great Depression meant that resources were limited, but Friedman patented a number of different designs.

The various machines had some things in common. There was a typewriter keyboard for the operator to enter the plaintext of a message, a series of rotors, and a printer for producing the ciphertext characters of the encrypted message.

The SIGABA machine above, also known as the ECMII, was theoretically similar to the Enigma and was used by the US government from the 1930s to the 1950s.

Crucial to the design was a system for generating a pseudorandom key that was separate from the machine itself, Kerckhoff's second principle. Friedman envisaged a loop of paper tape that would advance the rotors in an unpredictable manner, making it virtually impossible for cryptanalysts to break, even if they had details of how the machine was built. It proved troublesome to make the paper tape mechanism work in practice, and Friedman's assistant Frank Rowlett eventually convinced him that a design involving an extra set of rotors could do the job. The final design was detailed in a US patent in 1944 but was only publicly revealed in 2001.

Unusually, the device was used by both the US Army, where it was known as SIGABA, and the Navy, where it was called ECMII.

A British cipher machine called TypeX, developed by Wing Commander O G W Lywood, which was an adapted version of the commercial Enigma machine (see pages 130–131) could be used interoperably with SIGABA to exchange secure messages.

The cryptological strength of SIGABA came from the way the rotors moved after each letter was encrypted. The Friedman/Rowlett design meant that the rotors stepped in a pseudorandom way each time, something that earlier cipher machines, such as the Hebern device, did not.

When a cipher machine like the Hebern stepped its rotors in a simple way each time, this weakness could be used by cryptanalysts to break messages.

Interviews with German and Japanese POWs and other sources after the war revealed that they had failed to break the SIGABA cipher. This gave the Allies, who managed to break the German Enigma cipher machines, an incredible military advantage, one which surely influenced the outcome of World War II.

Using the cipher

The SIGABA machine contained fifteen rotors: five cipher rotors, five control rotors and five index rotors which sat in a series of slots.

The cipher and control rotors were of the same design and could be inserted in their slots in a forward or backward orientation and in any order. Both rotors had two sets of 26 contacts, which were wired together in a random order.

The index rotors were smaller than the other two types and contained two sets of 10 contacts. The rotors could be placed in any order in the index rotor slots and were set in an initial position each day based on settings from a chart produced each month. Unlike the other rotors, these did not advance after each letter.

This design gave the SIGABA 14,950 possible initial settings. While SIGABA proved to be a hugely effective advance over mechanical cipher systems such as Enigma because of its use of a pseudorandom key, the machine was heavy and prone to breaking. As a result, it was not used widely in field situations, where other systems proved more practical in spite of offering a lower level of security.

HILL CIPHER

The Hill cipher, which uses linear algebra and number theory to achieve encryption, marked a shift to modern cryptographic methods.

American mathematician Lester Sanders Hill had an early interest in how to detect errors in telegraph transmissions, but while at Hunter College, New York, his thoughts turned to cryptography. His paper *Cryptography in an Algebraic Alphabet* marked a move away from the manual cryptographic methods of old toward mechanization through the use of algebra. This had been suggested previously but Hill's was the first scheme that could be used generally as well as being secure.

One of the reasons the Hill cipher proved useful is that small changes in the plaintext lead to substantial changes in the ciphertext. A single change of letter in the plaintext usually results in the change of every letter in the ciphertext. The Hill cipher is susceptible to attack in some cases. If a cryptanalyst obtains two messages that have been encrypted from the same plaintext but with different equations or matrices and the numeric equivalents of the letters are known or guessed, decryption is relatively easy.

Using the cipher

The Hill cipher is a polygraphic substitution cipher which uses linear algebra or number theory to encrypt groups of letters. We assign numeric values to each letter. His method was to then represent the encryption as a series of simultaneous equations.

Say we wish to encrypt the word Mississippi using a trigraphic substitution (i.e. one which works on groups of three letters at a time).

We first split the plaintext into groups of three and add a null character, **k**, to ensure we have a full set of three.

mis sis sip pik

To encrypt these trigraphs, we use a matrix or the following series of three simultaneous equations, as a key.

$$y_1 = 11x_1 + 0\,x_2 + 3\,x_3$$
$$y_2 = 9\,x_1 + 22\,x_2 + 0\,x_3$$
$$y_3 = 6\,x_1 + 7\,x_2 + 11\,x_3$$

The number of equations required is equal to the size of the letter groupings – in this case three. The coefficients in the equations (the numbers before the x_1, x_2 and x_3) are not chosen at random. In the language of number theory, the matrix of these coefficients must be invertible. We then assign numeric values to each letter:

Letter	a	B	C	D	e	G	g	H	I	J	k	L	m	N	o	p	q	R	s	T	u	V	w	x	y	z
Value	5	23	2	20	10	15	8	4	18	25	0	16	13	7	3	1	19	6	12	24	21	17	14	22	11	9

The first three letters give us $x_1=13$ (m), $x_2=18$ (i) and $x_3=12$ (s). Putting these values into the equation for y_1 gives us

$$(11 \times 13) + (0 \times 18) + (3 \times 12) = 179$$

But the Hill cipher method requires us to use modulo 26 arithmetic:

$$y_1 = 179 = 23 \bmod 26.$$

A look at the numerical values Hill uses in his example tells us **23** represents the letter **b**. We can also work out from these equations that y_2 is **q** and y_3 is **t**. We then move on to the next set of three letters and we eventually get the following ciphertext

bqt sei aep yfc

We can construct a series of simultaneous equations that are the inverse of those above to decrypt the message.

$$x_1 = 22\,y_1 + 9\,y_2 + 20\,y_3$$
$$x_2 = 17\,y_1 + 7\,y_2 + 19\,y_3$$
$$x_3 = 15\,y_1 + 19\,y_2 + 22\,y_3$$

However, using large groups of letters quickly becomes too difficult to calculate by hand and Hill and Louis Weisner eventually patented a more efficient machine that could carry out the encryption for groups of up to six letters (hexagraphs).

Scherbius Cipher Machine

In the 1920s, the Germans used an automated machine based on polyalphabetic substitution to encrypt commercial messages.

In 1928 Dr Arthur Scherbius patented a mechanical cipher machine that was later sold under the name Enigma. The machine was about the size of a desktop computer and included a keyboard and a series of 26 lamps, each showing a letter. When a key was pressed, a different lamp lit up, showing the corresponding ciphertext letter. To obtain the original message, the recipient simply carried out the same operation in reverse.

The complexity of cracking the cipher posed a formidable challenge. In 1932 the Polish cryptography agency, Biuro Szyfrów, recruited a trio of young Polish cryptologists – the mathematicians Marian Rejewski, Jerzy Rozycki, and Henryk Zygalski – for the task. The head of the bureau's German section instructed Rejewski to work on his own for several hours a day on the German Enigma I machine. He was not allowed to tell anyone, not even his colleagues, what he was working on. It was Rejewski who worked out how the wiring of the machine must be working.

Messages sent using Scherbius's machine began with the rotor settings, encrypted twice. The user's manual for the machine might say that, on the fourth of the month, the rotors should be set with the letters 'a', 'x' and 'n' uppermost. The operator would then begin a message with the six characters AXNAXN before continuing with the body of the message.

The use of repetition gave the Poles the break they needed. They realized that, for any given configuration of Scherbius's machine, any letter entered would be enciphered as a different letter. Because the machine was reversible, that enciphered letter would then be enciphered as the original letter used.

The Poles built their own machine, called the cyclometer, which could check the rotor sequences. Using it, they put together a catalogue of the characteristics of the rotors. This took a year, but eventually meant that they were able to work out the rotor settings on any given day within about 15 minutes, so breaking all messages encrypted by the Scherbius cipher machine.

A rotor from Dr Arthur Scherbius' mechanical cipher machine, later sold under the name Enigma. The entirety of this machine was the size of a modern desktop computer.

Using the cipher

Each cipher letter displayed by the Scherbius machine depended on complex internal circuitry. Inside the machine were three rotating cylinders or rotors, each with a complicated series of internal wirings and electrical contacts on their faces so that every different position of the rotor resulted in a different electrical connection between the keys and the lamps. When a key was pressed, the first rotor moved on by one position; after 26 positions of the first, the second rotor moved on one position, and after this moved 26 positions, the third rotor moved on. The initial positions of the rotors could also be changed. Both sender and recipient had to ensure that their machines were set up in the same initial position in order to encrypt and decrypt messages.

The underlying cipher scheme in the Scherbius cipher machine is a polyalphabetic substitution cipher (see pages 58–59) but with many more alphabets. With three rotors, there can be 26 x 26 x 26, or 17,576, possible initial positions. Using the machine is therefore like using a substitution cipher with this many different alphabets.

CODEBREAKERS OF HISTORY

ALAN TURING AND THE ENIGMA MACHINE

The pioneering English computer scientist, cryptanalyst and mathematician Alan Turing developed a number of inspired techniques for breaking German ciphers in World War II.

By the mid-1930s, the German armed forces were using Scherbius's machine regularly to encrypt their communications, unaware that it had been broken by Marian Rejewski at the Polish cryptography agency (see pages 128–129.) Yet, as the decade continued, the German military modified the machine to make it even more complex. They added a plugboard through which specific pairs of letters could be interchanged by inserting cables between the plugs (known as *steckers*). According to historians Frank Carter and John Gallehawk, the modifications meant there were 158 million million million possible different ways of setting up the machine.

Events overtook Marian Rejewski and his colleagues.

Alan Turing in 1951, a computer scientist and mathematician whose codebreaking work at Bletchley Park is credited with shortening the World War II by years.

With the impending invasion of Poland, they shared their work with British intelligence. Britain's codebreaking activities were spearheaded by the Government Code and Cypher School at a country house called Bletchley Park, staffed by mathematicians from the universities of Oxford and Cambridge, who were joined later by colleagues from the allied countries, including the United States.

Among those working at Bletchley Park was a young man who had been recruited from King's College, Cambridge, Alan Turing. In his time at

Cambridge, Turing had shown himself to be a hugely gifted mathematician, proving the so-called central limit theorem in his dissertation. He also produced a landmark paper on computable numbers, which included a description of theoretical devices which have become known as Turing machines. Turing machines subsequently provided the theoretical basis for the invention of computers.

Using the work of the Poles to gain a headstart, Bletchley Park codebreakers Alan Turing and Gordon Welchman invented an electrical device known as a bombe to work through the initial rotor positions in turn. The name was derived from the Polish *bomba*, but was in fact a totally different device.

Essential to the Bletchley Park approach was the ability to find a crib. Messages frequently began with the word 'secret,' while naval messages often included the weather and their position. One operator was particularly fond of using ist – the German word for 'is' – as his message setting. Breaking Enigma was as much about highlighting human frailties as technical ones.

The design of the bombe allowed its operators to check the 26 possible *stecker* partners of a given input letter simultaneously for each of the nearly 18,000 possible rotor settings. As it ran through these settings, if it came across a series of settings that corresponded with the crib, it stopped. Manual techniques, such as frequency analysis (see pages 30–35), were then used to test the rotor settings.

After the success of the bombe, Turing moved on to lead Bletchley Park's Hut 8, which dealt with Germany's naval enigma code. There he invented a statistical technique known as Banburismus, similar to Friedman's Index of Coincidence (see pages 85–87), which enabled Bletchley Park to break the naval code until 1943. By the end of the war, the Bletchley Park team had broken more than two and a half million Enigma messages and had made highly significant contributions to the Allied victory.

LORENZ SZ40

Germany's high command used an even more complex rotor machine to encrypt messages between Adolf Hitler and his generals. Yet Allied codebreakers managed to build a copy of the machine following an incredibly fortuitous breakthrough.

The Allies were quick to realize that the Hitler's messages were sent using a different machine, later discovered to be the Lorenz SZ40.

In August 1941, a German cipher operator made a seemingly innocent mistake. A long message was sent, but became corrupted in transmission. The operator resent the message using the same key but with a few of the words abbreviated. Both messages were intercepted and relayed to Bletchley Park. Two related ciphertexts are known in cryptology as a *depth*.

Bletchley Park's Brigadier John Tiltman then used these two ciphertexts to work out a long stretch of the key sequence. Incredibly, using this depth, the Allied cryptanalysts, led by mathematician Bill Tutte, were able to work out the basic design of the Lorenz machine by reverse engineering and to build their own version, which they called British Tunny.

Part of the problem was keeping two punched paper tapes travelling at high speed in synchronization. Bletchley Park's Cambridge mathematician Alan Turing suggested building a machine that replaced one of the paper tapes with a series of valves that acted like digital switches, eliminating the synchronization problems. It took ten months and 1500 valves to build the machine, known as Colossus, which was installed and began work at Bletchley Park in December 1943.

Colossus was the size of a room and weighed a ton, but the valve technology meant that Colossus could crack a Lorenz-encrypted message in hours. By the end of the war, ten Colossi with an even higher number of valves were in use at Bletchley Park. Hitler's most secret messages were no longer safe.

Using the cipher

The SZ in the Lorenz machine name stood for *Schlüsselzusatz*, or additive key, and this gives the basis on which the machine encrypted its text. The

The Colossus was installed at Bletchley Park in December 1943. It could crack a German code in a matter of hours and was the brainchild of Alan Turing.

machine represented letters using a five-character long string of zeros and ones. For example, the letter 'a' was **11000** while 'l' was **01001**.

Each letter was encrypted by combining its binary representation with the representation of another letter using an operation known as exclusive-or (see pages 150–151).

The key to the Lorenz machine's complexity was the seeming randomness of the added letter, generated by those 12 rotors known as a Vernam stream cipher. As with Enigma, the Lorenz machine's rotors rotated after each letter. Five of them rotated in a regular manner while five rotated according to the settings of two pinwheels. Breaking the messages thus relied on finding the correct initial rotor settings.

In 1942, the German high command eventually introduced enhanced versions of the Lorenz machine. Had the Lorenz machines been used correctly, their ciphertext would have been virtually impossible to crack, but the Allies used a backdoor to help them understand what strategies Hitler was telling his generals to pursue.

POEM CODE

In 1940, Britain established the secretive Special Operations
Executive (SOE) to carry out spying and sabotage missions in
occupied Europe and to help regional resistance movements.
They used a system known as the Poem Code to encipher
their messages.

At its height, approximately 13,000 people were involved with the SOE's work.
To communicate with its agents behind enemy lines, the SOE had adopted
the poem code. When the SOE employed a cryptographer, Leo Marks, to
have oversight of communication, he soon realized that it was not quite as
undecipherable as the SOE imagined.

In his memoir *Between Silk and Cyanide*, Marks says poem codes had been
adopted by the SOE 'because of a theory, traditional in Intelligence, that if an
agent were caught and searched it was better security if his code was in his
head.' Marks had a gut feeling that this was wrong.

Marks also says that the SOE's country heads were in the habit of sending
the same message with only minor changes from several different agents in
the belief that this would mean the message got through. In fact, all it did was
make it easier for the Germans to crack.

Another problem was that because agents had to be able to remember the
poem, they often used popular ones. Marks says that the works of Shakespeare,
Tennyson, and the Bible were often used. The Germans knew this and often
tried well-known poems to see if one of them produced readable messages.
If German codebreakers were able to break just one message then all others
produced using the same code could easily be reconstructed. It was for this
reason that Marks eventually convinced the SOE to stop using poem codes.

He persuaded the SOE to replace them with what were called 'worked
out keys'. The code would still be based on transposition but the keys were
generated randomly. Both sender and recipient would have an identical copy
of this list of keys, printed on a piece of silk. As each key on the list was used,
that piece of silk was cut off and burned.

Using the code

The first step is to have a poem memorized. It does not need to be particularly long. For instance, let us take William Shakespeare's Sonnet 18 – 'Shall I compare thee to a Summer's day? Thou art more lovely and more temperate.'

We then choose five words from this, say, 'compare', 'day', 'lovely', 'more' and 'temperate' and write them out in a grid.

We then work our way through the alphabet, starting at 'a' and find the first occurrence, numbering it 1. The second 'a' is numbered 2, the third 3. We then move to the letter 'b' and do the same. If no 'b' is found, we just move on to 'c' and continue numbering in this way.

c	o	m	p	a	r	e	d	a	y	l	o	v	e	l	y	m	o	r	e	t	e	m	p	e	r	a	t	e
4	17	14	20	1	22	6	5	2	28	12	18	27	7	13	29	15	19	23	8	25	9	16	21	10	24	3	26	11

When encrypting a message, we use the transcription key above to transpose the plaintext.

This key has 29 letters. To encrypt a message using it, we write out the plaintext in a grid of rows of that same number of letters. We pad out the message with null characters to fill the final row.

We then use the numbers in the transcription key. In our case the first number is 4 so we write out all of the letters in column 4. This continues with the letters in column 17 and 14 and so on, creating the ciphertext. In reality, two transcriptions might be used to convolute the message further.

One of the problems with the poem code is that errors were commonly made in encoding and this would render a message unreadable. SOE codebreaker Leo Marks claims that as much as 20 per cent of the SOE's traffic could not be read because of agents' errors.

PURPLE CIPHER AND PEARL HARBOR

A machine known as Purple encrypted messages sent by Japan's military leaders during World War II. America's cryptanalysts broke its code, but this was not enough to stop the destruction at Pearl Harbor.

In 1938, for its high-level diplomatic messages, Japan started using a machine known as the *97-shiki obun Inji-ki*, which took input in the form of Latin characters rather than Japanese *katakana* characters. This machine became known to American codebreakers as Purple, following their tradition of naming Japanese ciphers after colours.

The Purple cipher was a polyalphabetic substitution cipher, and the number of alphabets it used was enormous, making methods such as frequency analysis (see pages 30–35), too time-consuming. Unlike Enigma, Purple did not use rotors, but stepping switches similar to those found in telephone exchanges. Each switch had 25

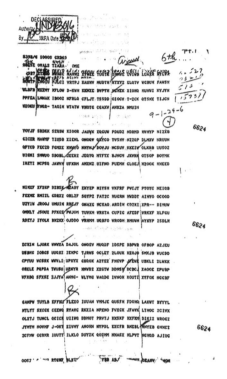

A part of the encrypted message sent on 7 December 1941 relating to the Pearl Harbor attack, although this was not realized in time.

positions and stepped to the next position when an electric pulse was applied. Inside the machine, the alphabet was divided into two groups, one of six letters (the vowels plus the letter 'y') and one of twenty letters (the consonants).

For the vowels, there was a switch that stepped once for each character input. However, there were three connected 25-position switches for the consonants, rotating like the odometer on a car.

Cracking the cipher

The Japanese believed that the Purple cipher was unbreakable. However, a team at the US Army Signals Intelligence Service (SIS), led by the service's chief William F Friedman and cryptanalyst Frank Rowlett, managed it. Perhaps the biggest advance in breaking Purple was made by SIS's Leo Rosen, who managed to build a replica of the Japanese machine. Astonishingly, when a fragment of one of the machines was found at the Japanese Embassy in Berlin at the end of the war, it turned out that Rosen had used exactly the same stepping switch in his replica – an inspired guess indeed.

The cryptanalytical techniques used in breaking Purple were similar to those used in breaking the Enigma cipher. Frequently used salutations and closing remarks were used as cribs, while messages that had been transmitted more than once in error were used to crack this 'uncrackable' cipher.

Cracking the basis of Purple did not mean that every message was instantly readable – there were still the message keys to uncover – so intelligence flowing from SIS's breakthrough was at best patchy. There was also the problem of distributing intelligence gained from reading encrypted messages. Because of the necessary secrecy involved, many who received the intelligence did not recognize its value.

In addition, many codebreaking experts believe that the ability of the US to read some Purple messages led to complacency that was to be brutally shattered just a few years later. On 7 December 1941, a Purple-encrypted message intercepted from the Japanese Embassy breaking off diplomatic relations with the US was decrypted, but the message did not reach the US State Department in enough time for them to realize that it related to the forthcoming attack on Pearl Harbor. However, there was no specific reference to the attack in the message, so it seems unlikely that anything could have been done in time in any case.

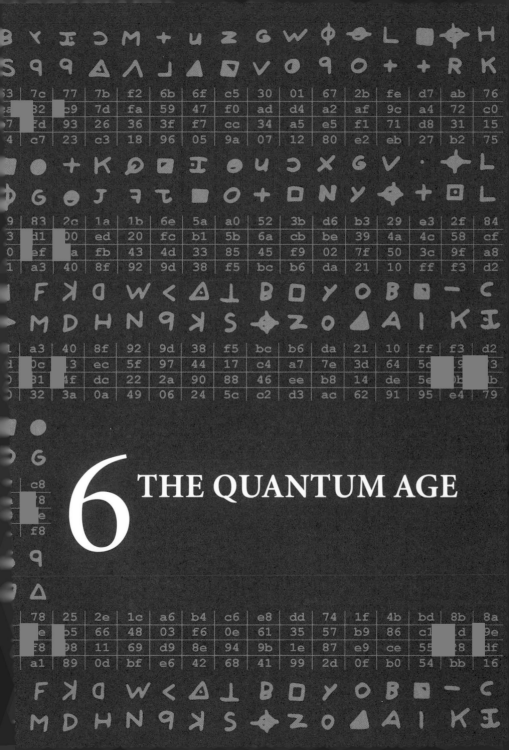

6 THE QUANTUM AGE

CODING IN THE DIGITAL ERA

The advent of the computer changed cryptology forever. The success of cipher machines like Enigma and SIGABA relied on the complexity of their inner workings. A programmable computer could create such intricacies in software, dramatically simplifying the encryption process.

At the same time, cryptanalysts gained a new weapon in their armoury. Ciphers that had been too hard to crack because they needed too much time to analyze suddenly became child's play. Brute-force attacks, where every possible key is tried in order to find the correct one, were suddenly plausible thanks to the muscle of technology.

The creation of the Internet and World Wide Web, shrinking the planet even more and shifting many things that happened in the real world of bricks and mortar to a virtual one, has also led to an increased need for the security provided by codes and ciphers. Billions of people now use encryption every day of their lives when checking their bank balance, sending an email or simply visiting a website.

The SZ42, a later version of the Lorenz SZ40, which Adolf Hitler used to send messages.

As a result, cracking codes now is generally about having the fastest computers rather than merely being an interested amateur, who must now turn his or her attention to the unsolved ciphers of earlier times for their pleasure.

The National Security Agency bought the world's first Cray supercomputer in 1974 and in 2013 began construction of a near $900 million supercomputing center at Fort Meade, Maryland.

Being a good eavesdropper has always been a helpful trait for the successful cryptanalyst, whether intercepting letters from royalty or listening in to German Morse code signals. One of the biggest revelations from whistleblower Edward Snowden was that the NSA and GCHQ have a program called Tempora that involves tapping into what is passing through the world's fiber-optic cable network.

As we stand here in the early years of the third millennium CE, it is easy to think that the 5,000-year war between cryptologists and cryptanalysts is coming to an end, with those writing coded messages emerging as the winners, handed their victory by technology, mathematics and even quantum mechanics.

Quantum cryptography potentially offers a truly unbreakable method of encryption. But quantum mechanics does not tell us everything about the world, and future advances in physics may further complicate the picture, by providing new methods of both encryption and codebreaking.

As more and more messages are sent using seemingly unbreakable ciphers, the focus inevitably swings back to the weakest links in any chain of communication – the people themselves. While computers and quantum particles cannot be bribed or blackmailed to reveal their information, people can. Rather than trying to decrypt the message itself, why not just place a spy within the company providing the encryption or surreptitiously install a keylogger on their computer?

Digital Steganography

The technique of steganography, or hiding messages, can be brought right up to date with the use of digital rather than physical messages. While traditional steganography made use of invisible inks on paper and tattoos on shaved heads, digital steganography hides messages in the binary digits that are used to represent images, audio and emails. The primary advantage of steganography across the centuries is that it can conceal not only the message but the fact that a message is being sent at all.

With Google alone handling 100 petabytes of data every day, hiding messages in that tsunami of data seems perfect. One widely explored method is the use of a spam email to conceal information. However, the more promising path for modern steganographers is the use of images.

Using the cipher

Imagine a grid of squares, say 5x5. We can draw a simple image on that grid by changing some squares black as shown below.

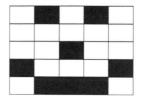

We can represent this image digitally by using zeroes to represent white squares and ones to represent the black ones. In digital systems, these squares are usually called pixels (picture elements). Thus the image can be represented as **01010, 00000, 00100, 10001, 01110**. Colour digital images are represented in a similar way, but instead of using '**0**'s and '**1**'s, we have to use a wider range of numbers to represent various colours.

In the digital image system known as 24-bit RGB (red-green-blue), which can be used to distinguish between millions of different shades, the red, green and blue contributions to each pixel are represented by eight binary digits. The contributions range from no colour (**00000000**) to full colour (**11111111**).

If we consider just the blue contribution for a moment, the difference in shades represented by **11111110** and **11111111** is imperceptible to the human eye. Knowing this we can use the rightmost digit to hide information. One pixel will give us three binary digits (red, green and blue) to play with; a web image measuring 5cm (2in) square contains more than 20,000 pixels, so you can easily hide a text message or even a completely different picture, as long as the recipient knows how to extract the information.

The picture opposite shows how this works. The cat image on the left has had the message image subtly added to it to create the new cat image on the right. To the naked eye, they are identical but the middle image has been hidden in the colour information of the right image, altering the shades subtly.

The least significant bits of sound files can be used in a similar way – small changes to each note are impossible for a listener to perceive but they can hide secret information.

The similarity of the two cat images might make us think it is impossible to crack digital steganography. However, there are techniques we can use. If we have intercepted the cat image on the right and we scour the Internet for the original image, we could be in with a chance of extracting the hidden message by subtracting the pixel information in one from the other.

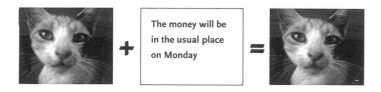

We can also carry out what is known as a statistical attack on the intercepted image to guess what might have happened. In an unencrypted image, we can reasonably expect that the final binary digit of each component to be **0** half the time and **1** half the time. Hiding a message in those digits will alter this statistic and could lead us to believe that digital steganography has been used.

D'AGAPEYEFF CIPHER

A cipher posed as a challenge in a book about the history of cryptography has kept codebreakers guessing since it was published 77 years ago.

Just as World War II was about to break out, Alexander D'Agapeyeff published a book called *Codes and Ciphers* which included 'a cryptogram upon which the reader is invited to test his skill'. Despite numerous attempts to solve it, it remains unsolved.

The cryptogram is as follows:

75628 28591 62916 48164 91748 58464 74748 28483 81638 18174
74826 26475 83828 49175 74658 37575 75936 36565 81638 17585
75756 46282 92857 46382 75748 38165 81848 56485 64858 56382
72628 36281 81728 16463 75828 16483 63828 58163 63630 47481
91918 46385 84656 48565 62946 26285 91859 17491 72756 46575
71658 36264 74818 28462 82649 18193 65626 48484 91838 57491
81657 27483 83858 28364 62726 26562 83759 27263 82827 27283
82858 47582 81837 28462 82837 58164 75748 58162 92000

The most immediate thing to jump out of the D'Agapeyeff cipher is the fact that alternate columns only include either the digits 6, 7, 8, 9 and 0 or the digits 1, 2, 3, 4 and 5, except at the very end of the cryptogram where three zeros appear together.

Most of those who have tried to solve the cipher have used this information to suggest that it is a Polybius square (see pages 24–27) and that null characters (the final zeros) are used to pad out the square. Polybius squares are featured heavily in the D'Agapeyeff book so this method of attack seems logical.

A Polybius square that could use this method is shown below:

	1	2	3	4	5
6	A	B	C	D	E
7	F	G	H	I/J	K
8	L	M	N	O	P
9	Q	R	S	T	U
0	V	W	X	Y	Z

With this, the plaintext message

FLEE, WE ARE DISCOVERED

would be encrypted as

71 81 65 65 02 65 61 92 65 64 74 93 63 84 01 65 92 65 64

Written as groups of five this gives

71816 56502 65619 26564 74936 38401 65926 56400

which we have padded out with null zeros at the end to make it look very similar to the D'Agapeyeff cipher.

	1	2	3	4	5
6	0	17	12	16	11
/	1	9	0	14	17
8	20	17	15	11	17
9	12	3	2	1	0
0	0	0	0	1	0

If we do a frequency analysis of the individual digit pairs, the resulting table looks like there is a natural language behind it, perhaps even English.

Yet the problem a cryptanalyst faces is that there are many more occurrences of these symbols appearing in pairs or even triples than you would expect if the language were English. For example, the pair 75 appears three times in a row. Words with repeated triple letters are rare, although the triples could arise from adjoining words such as 'tell like'.

The mystery has taken on an extra twist in that these editions of the book, from 1952, appear without the mystery cryptogram. Some have suggested that the deletion of the cryptogram from later editions is because the cipher is actually a dictionary code based on the 3rd edition of the Concise Oxford Dictionary which was replaced by the 4th edition in 1952. In 1955 D'Agapeyeff died, taking the secret of his cipher with him.

VIC CIPHER

A simple substitution cipher can be made more complex by using variable length ciphertext substitutions, as is the case with this Soviet-era system.

The VIC cipher is one of a class called straddling checkerboard ciphers which use a technique called fractionation to make a simple substitution cipher more complex. The VIC cipher was used by the Soviets during the Cold War and is one of the most complicated ciphers ever used in the field where encryption is carried out manually. The VIC cipher is named for victor, the codename used by the Leningrad-born Reino Häyhänen, who used it and who later defected to the United States.

Cracking the cipher

The story of how the VIC cipher was cracked has an unusual beginning. In June 1953, a delivery boy for the *Brooklyn Eagle* was given change for a dollar. He dropped one of the nickels and, to his surprise, it fell apart, revealing a tiny photograph showing a series of numbers at its center.

The FBI could make no headway in understanding what the numbers meant until, in 1957, they had a breakthrough. A 36-year-old lieutenant colonel from the KGB handed himself in at the US Embassy in Paris, saying he was an officer

One of the original encrypted messages sent by Rudolf Abel, a Soviet spy who was welcoming another spy into the US.

in the Soviet intelligence service. The spy, Reino Häyhänen, revealed that he had entered the US in 1951, and had taken on the identity of an Idaho-born man with Estonian parents.

During a search of Häyhänen's house, the FBI found another hollow coin containing a similar photograph. When questioned, Häyhänen revealed details of the encryption method and the message on the photograph was revealed. The nickel had been intended for Häyhänen on his arrival in the US and was nothing more than a welcome message. Häyhänen then collaborated with the FBI to unmask Soviet spy Rudolf Ivanovich Abel. Abel was sentenced to 45 years in prison for his spying, but was handed back to the Soviet Union in exchange for US spy plane pilot Gary Powers.

Using the cipher

A straddling checkerboard cipher uses a key phrase and two numbers – for example, the 'thequickbrownfxjmpdvlazysg' and the numbers 5 and 7. The key is written in a 3x10 grid with the columns numbered with the digits 0 to 9 by placing nothing in the cell in the first column of the top row of letters, and starting each of the subsequent rows with one of the chosen numbers. Generally the top row will contain the most commonly used eight letters and two spaces, while the bottom rows will also contain two spaces. To encrypt a character, the sender replaces the plaintext with the column number for letters in the top row, and the row number followed by the column number for the two subsequent. For example, the plaintext 'Meet me in Central Park' would become: **58 2 2 0 58 2 6 54 8 2 54 0 51 73 72 59 73 51 9**. The digits are then run together and divided into groups of five to make decryption harder.

The VIC cipher used a more complicated version of this code, employing additional steps to generate a different order for the numbers in the top row of the grid, adding nulls, and also involving another two additional transpositions.

CODEBREAKERS OF HISTORY

DONALD HARDEN

Between 1966 and 1974, police in California were stumped by a series of murders, apparently perpetrated by the same person. The victims were aged between 16 and 29.

In 1969, someone with knowledge that only the murderer and the police could have had began writing to local newspapers, demanding that they print a series of four encrypted messages on their front pages. The writer of the coded messages said he or she had killed 37 people, although the police have only ever confirmed seven of these. The writer also said that the coded messages would explain the motives behind the killings; they were also to reveal the identity of the killer, known as the Zodiac Killer.

On 1 August 1969, the *San Francisco Chronicle*, *San Francisco Examiner*, and the *Vallejo Times-Herald* received almost identical letters, each of them containing a different part of a 408-symbol cryptogram that became known as the 'three-part cipher'.

Two months later, a taxi driver called Paul Stine was shot dead by a passenger on his way to Presidio Heights in San Francisco. On 8 November, the killer mailed another cryptogram, which has become known as the '340 cipher,' referring to the number of symbols it contains. The Zodiac Killer continued to correspond with the newspapers in 1970 and in one letter wrote 'My name is,' followed by a 13-character cipher. The killer often used the fourth symbol of this cipher – a circle with a cross in it – to sign off his or her letters.

A page of one of the encrypted series of letters sent to the Californian press from the 'Zodiac Killer', who claimed to have killed 37 people between 1966 and 1974.

Communications ceased without warning in 1974 and the killer has never been found or definitively identified.

The three-part cipher contained around fifty different symbols, some of them similar to those used to represent signs of the Zodiac. The text of the 340 cipher, meanwhile, contained 63 different characters. The multitude of characters means that neither is a simple substitution cipher.

In 1969 teacher Donald Harden and his wife Bettye managed to crack the three-part cipher. They realized that it was a homophonic substitution cipher (see pages 62–65), with several symbols representing the same plaintext character. In cracking the cipher, the couple had assumed that the killer would have egotistically started the message with 'I' and that the message would contain the words 'kill' or 'killing'. They were proven to be right.

However, the three-part cipher held yet another mystery. At the end, the message ended with the garbled string of characters 'EBEORIETEMETHHPITI'. If written in a homophonic cipher, then it is a different one from the main text. Some believe that the string of characters might reveal the identity of the killer or represents a key for the later 340 cipher. Many have tried to decrypt the 340 cipher and the 'My name is' cryptogram but all of the solutions that have been publicized rely on tortuous logic, such as using anagrams and misspelt words, to get to a plaintext. The likelihood is that the Zodiac Killer's cipher has not yet been cracked and that the mystery remains.

The Zodiac Killer ciphers website (www.zodiackillerciphers.com) has a useful list of many proposed solutions under the title 'Discredited or inconclusive solution attempts,' and also gives the reasons why they have been discredited. The fact that other unbroken codes and ciphers have eventually been discovered after many years of trying means that more codebreakers will try their hands at the Zodiac ciphers. The thought that they may finally bring a killer to justice is also very appealing.

BLOCK CIPHERS

1976

The advent of computers after World War II led to increasing automation of cipher systems. One of the most widely used systems is based on performing complex cycles of transformations on the binary digits of plaintext characters.

In the early 1970s, the US National Bureau of Standards (NBS) sought a method of encrypting governmental information that was sensitive but not top secret. They wanted something simple, fast, and cost-effective. A team at IBM, headed up by Horst Feistel, developed the Data Encryption Standard (DES), based on what is known as a block cipher, where the output from a product cipher (a cipher combining multiple transformations) is fed back into itself in an iteration loop. DES was adopted in 1976 and used successfully for more than twenty years, but its weaknesses were exposed by increasing computational power.

Attempts to break DES typically focus on what are known as brute-force attacks. DES has 72,057,594,037,927,936 possible keys, yet checking those by hand would be unfeasible. In 1998, the Electronic Frontier Foundation spent a quarter of a million dollars building a computer called DES Cracker containing more than 1,500 chips; it cracked DES in just two days.

		Middle bits															
		0000	0001	0010	0011	0100	0101	0110	0111	1000	1001	1100	1011	1100	1101	1101	1111
Outside bits	00	0010	1100	0100	0001	0111	1100	1011	0110	1000	0101	0011	1111	1101	0000	1110	1001
	01	1110	1011	0010	1100	0100	0111	1101	0001	0101	0000	1111	1100	0011	1001	1000	0110
	10	0100	0010	0001	1011	1100	1101	0111	1000	1111	1001	1100	0101	0110	0011	0000	1110
	11	1011	1000	1100	0111	0001	1110	0010	1101	0110	1111	0000	1001	1100	0100	0101	0011

Using the cipher

In a block cipher, the message to be encrypted is broken down into blocks of the same fixed length. In the case of DES, these blocks are 64 bits long – this is because this is the length that the hardware at the time could handle most effectively.

The cipher uses an exclusive-or (XOR) operation:

Binary input 1	Binary input 2	Output
0	0	0
0	1	1
1	0	1
1	1	0

The exclusive-or operation takes two binary digits as inputs. If the input digits are the same then the output is the binary digit zero; if they are different then the output is the binary digit one. The operation is used widely in modern cryptography.

To encrypt a message, the plaintext blocks undergo 16 rounds of processing. In each round, the 64-bit block is divided into left- and right-hand halves, each 32 bits long, and a 48-bit-long subkey is generated from a secret key. The right-hand half of the block is then expanded to 48 bits long by duplicating some of the binary digits. This is combined using an exclusive-or function with the subkey. The resulting 48-bit number is then divided into eight blocks of six binary digits. Each of these eight blocks passes through something called a substitution- or S-box to reduce it back down to four bits. Each of the eight S-boxes is different. For example, if the six-digit input is **011011**, the output from the fifth S-box is revealed in the table opposite. The middle four bits of the input are **1101** so we scan down that column and look across the row where the outer bits are **01**. The output from the S-box is highlighted, **1001**.

· The eight blocks of four digits are strung back together to get a 32-bit long number. This new number is then combined with the left-hand half of the original, using the exclusive-or operation. The left- and right-hand halves are now switched over and we start on the next round. Eventually, all 16 rounds are completed and the original input has been completely jumbled up.

PUBLIC-KEY ENCRYPTION (PKE)

One of the big challenges of using a key to make a cipher more secure is the difficulty of exchanging them safely between sender and recipient.

A system of key encryption was developed by Britain's Government Communications Headquarters (GCHQ), the organization that grew out of the work of Bletchley Park; Whitfield Diffie and Martin Hellman at Stanford University also addressed this issue.

Public-key encryption (PKE) is an asymmetric key cipher in which different keys are used to encrypt and decrypt a message. Ronald Rivest, Adi Shamir, and Leonard Adleman – three researchers at Massachusetts Institute of Technology – worked out a way to use very large prime numbers (those that can only be divided by themselves and one) to use PKE in practice. They founded a company, RSA Encryption, and the system that they developed is now used by billions of people worldwide, when banking online or sending an email, for example.

The RSA system works by using two very large prime numbers that have been multiplied together as one of the keys. The widely used software Pretty Good Privacy (PGP) uses public-key encrpytion, along with some other encryption methods, to encrypt emails.

The security of PKE lies in how difficult it is for eavesdroppers to work out the mathematical relationship between the public and private keys. Multiplying two prime numbers together is a relatively trivial task. However, doing the reverse, knowing the answer and trying to work out the two numbers that have been multiplied together – a process called factorization – takes a very long time.

Brute-force methods for factoring large numbers take too much time and effort. RSA themselves say, 'Factoring 100-digit numbers is easy with today's hardware and algorithms. No public effort has yet resulted in successful factoring of numbers of more than 200 digits.' There are shortcuts. Cryptanalysts sometimes use a piece of algebra called the elliptic curve method to find factors by solving the equation $y^2 = x^3 + ax + b$.

Factors are found by using points on these curves and using the mathematics of group theory. Sieve methods are used for bigger numbers. With these, all of the multiples of smaller numbers in succession are excluded from the search in turn to reduce the number of factors that you ultimately have to check.

The weak link in all PKE systems is their potential vulnerability to faster methods of working out the mathematical link between the keys. Although finding prime factors is currently too time-consuming, there is the possibility that a new mathematical shortcut might be discovered to make the process simple. Computing power might also increase at a faster rate than expected; some believe that quantum computers could easily solve factorization problems that are currently unfeasible.

Using the cipher

PKE works using a pair of keys – one that is public and one that is kept secret. The public key is often held on a central server that anyone can access. Crucially, the two keys are connected via a mathematical relationship.

Say Bob wants to send Alice a message. Bob uses Alice's public key from the server to encrypt her message. Alice then uses her private key to decrypt the message. The beauty of the system is that if an eavesdropper, Eve, intercepts Bob's message, she does not have access to Alice's private key and is therefore unable to recreate the original plaintext.

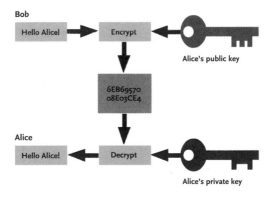

A visual representation of the Public-key encryption, which was developed by Britain's Government Communications Headquarters.

WIFI CIPHERS

Many people come into contact with encryption on a daily basis without actually realizing it. When we connect to a wireless hotspot we usually do so using a secure connection. So how is the connection made secure? The answer is a stream cipher.

If you imagine the data that flows across a wireless connection as a string of binary digits (bits) then a stream cipher encrypts these one at a time by performing a mathematical operation on each digit with another digit from an infinitely long key.

Instead of using a truly random key like the one-time pad, a stream cipher uses a pseudorandom key – one that has been generated mathematically but is random enough to satisfy statistical tests. The result is a cipher that is less secure but that can be used in practical applications. Stream ciphers began to be used from 1999 in the 802.11b WiFi standard called WEP or Wired Equivalent Privacy. WEP was based on a stream cipher called RC4 invented by Ron Rivest, one of the inventors of the RSA algorithm.

WEP's fall from grace came about because it was recognized that information about the key was leaking into messages. In 2001, cryptographers Fluhrer, Mantin and Shamir published a paper which detailed how an attacker could simply collect a large number of messages encrypted using RC4 to eventually discover the key. This weakness was exploited in hacking tools such as AirSnort.

It was this that led to the introduction of WPA or WiFi Protected Access. WPA is still based on the RC4 cipher – this meant that existing wireless hardware could still be used with a firmware upgrade – but is combined with a new regime for key generation called Temporal Key Integrity Protocol (TKIP). TKIP changes the master key for every 10,000 packets. This meant that hackers were unable to collect enough ciphertext messages to work out the original key.

When RC4 is used as a WiFi cipher, it uses either a 64-bit or 128-bit seed. In 64-bit, the user enters a ten-digit passcode in hexadecimal characters (0 to 9 and A to F) which equates to 40 bits and is combined with a 24-bit initialization vector (IV) which is different for each data packet sent over the wireless connection. In 128-bit WEP, the user enters a 26 character long hexadecimal string which is combined with the IV.

This seed is then fed into the RC4 algorithm, which generates an infinite pseudorandom string of bits. The algorithm creates an array S which is stepped through 256 iterations. For each iteration, two specified values in the array are swapped and the sum of their contents used to point to a third element. The contents of that element then provide the output stream. To create the ciphertext, each bit of this stream undergoes an exclusive-or operation with each bit of the plaintext. This process is shown below:

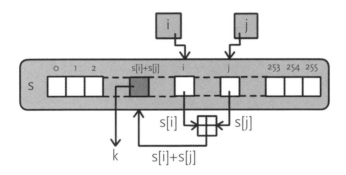

WPA eventually proved vulnerable to other types of attack, notably a message integrity code key attack. In this, the code used to check that a message has not been garbled in communication is used to reveal the key.

SOLITAIRE CIPHER

New Yorker Bruce Schneier is one of the world's leading cryptographers and has invented or co-invented a number of cryptographic algorthms including the Solitaire cipher.

This was created specifically as a plot device for the 1999 Neal Stephenson code-breaking themed novel *Cryptonomicon*. Schneier was born in New York in 1963 and studied physics at the Univeristy of Rochester before taking a master's degree in computer science at the American University in Washington DC. As well as working actively in the sector (as chief technology officer of cybersecurity firm Resilient Systems) he has also written and spoken extensively about cryptographic methods.

Using the cipher

Schneier says, 'An agent might be in a situation where he just does not have access to a computer, or may be prosecuted if he has tools for secret communication. But a deck of cards ... what harm is that?'

The cipher uses a pack of 52 playing cards plus two non-identical jokers, which we will call **A** and **B**. The deck should be shuffled and a second pack ordered in an identical manner given to the recipient.

Now take the pack of cards face up in your hand and find the **A** joker and swap it with the card beneath it. If the **A** joker is at the bottom, move it below the top card. Now find the **B** joker and move it two cards down. If the **B** joker is at the bottom, move it below the second card. If it is one up from the bottom, move it below the top card. This process must be done in order.

So if the deck looks like this before step 1:

A 7 2 B 9 4 1

at the end of step 2 it should look like:

7 A 2 9 4 B 1

Now swap the cards above the joker highest in the pack with the cards below the lowest. If the deck looks like this:

2 4 6 B 5 8 7 1 A 3 9

then after this step it will look like this:

3 9 B 5 8 7 1 A 2 4 6

Take the bottom card from the deck and put it to one side. If it is a club, it is the value shown (with Jack worth 11, Queen 12 and King 13). If the card is a diamond, it is the value plus 13. If it is a heart, it is the value plus 26. If it is a spade, it is the value plus 39. Either joker is a 53.

Count that number down from the top card and cut the cards there, putting the lower cards on top of the upper cards. Put the bottom card back on the bottom.

Now look at the top card and convert it to a number in the same manner as above. Count down that many cards (starting with one for the top card) and then look at the card after the number you counted down. This is known as the output card. If it is a joker, you need to start the process again from the point that you found the **A** and **B** jokes above.

If it is not, we convert this card to a number but in a slightly different way. If it is a club, it is the value shown (with Jack worth 11, Queen 12 and King 13). If the card is a diamond, it is the value plus 13. If it is a heart, it is the value. If it is a spade, it is the value plus 13.

To use Solitaire to encrypt a plaintext message, we take each character and convert it to a number, its position in the alphabet, i.e. **A=1 ... Z=26**.

We then take the output card number and add it to this position number. If the sum is higher than 26, we subtract 26 (in the style of modulo 26 arithmetic). We then convert this number back into a letter. If we added 9 and 27 to get 36, then subtracted 26 to get 10, the ciphertext letter would be **J**. We then repeat the whole process with the deck of cards to get a second output card to add to the second plaintext character. We carry on until we have encrypted each letter of the message.

To decipher the message, the recipient reverses the process.

ADVANCED ENCRYPTION STANDARD

In the mid-1970s, America's National Bureau of Standards (NBS) invited submissions from interested parties for ideas on how to encrypt uncensored but sensitive government data.

Computer firm IBM submitted an idea for using a symmetric block cipher, a cipher that works on blocks of data of fixed length and uses the same key for encryption and decryption. In 1977, an updated version of the cipher, called the Data Encryption Standard or DES, was published and quickly adopted.

DES used a block size of 64 bits and a key of the same size, although only 56 bits of the key were used for cryptographic purposes with the remainder being used to reduce the likelihood of errors in transmission.

In response to the security company RSA offering rewards to organizations and individuals who could crack the DES cipher, the Electronic Frontier Foundation (EFF) had already shown that their DES cracker (nicknamed 'Deep Crack') could use a brute-force attack to quickly go through all 2^{56} possible keys (see page 150). In 1999 the EFF demonstrated that this could now be done in less than a day.An upgraded version of DES, called Triple DES, was adopted that year but DES was eventually shown to be insecure against the increased computer processing power available, and was replaced by the Advanced Encryption Standard (AES) in 2002.

There is currently no publicly known attack on AES which would allow eavesdroppers to read messages encrypted using the algorithm. That said, a number of theoretical attacks on AES have been published which would allow a message to be decrypted faster than a full brute-force attack. However, the amount of time required to fulfil such an attack would be practically unfeasible. Revelations by former National Security contractor Edward Snowden, as reported in the *Washington Post* in 2014, show that the NSA, as part of its Penetrating Hard Targets program is looking at new methods of breaking AES, including the development of powerful quantum computers.

Using the cipher

AES is a symmetric block cipher based on an algorithm submitted to the National Institute of Standard and Technology or NIST (which replaced the NBS) by two Belgian cryptographers, Joan Daemen and Vincent Rijmen.

It is an encryption standard designed to encrypt blocks of 128-bit long data (meaning that it transforms 128 characters of plaintext into 128 characters of ciphertext.) To do this it uses 128-, 192- or 256-bit long keys, known as AES-128, AES-192 and AES-256. (The larger keys are used to provide higher levels of encryption.)

The algorithm operates on a matrix of 16 eight-bit bytes, which undergoes repeated transformations, the number of repetitions depending on the length of the key: 10 cycles for a 128-bit key, 12 for 192 and 14 for 256.

For each cycle, the key is scrambled and combined with the matrix of input data using an XOR operation (see page 150–151). This is followed by a transformation step called SubBytes, which transforms bytes by using a substitution box. A process called ShiftRows is then applied to the matrix. This shifts the bytes in the second row one place to the left, the third row by two places and the fourth row by three places. Then the bytes within each column are transformed through a process called MixColumns, which considers each column as a polynomial equation and multiplies the columns by a fixed matrix. (This step is omitted in the last round.) In the final transformation, the bytes are combined with elements of the expanded key using an XOR operation.

The ciphertext that is output from this process has been scrambled in a way that is sufficiently mathematically complex to make it extremely hard to subject it to a brute-force attack. The challenge for future encryption systems will to be keep producing systems such as this that are far enough ahead of current cryptanalysis to resist the ongoing challenge of the codebreakers.

SECURE HASH ALGORITHM

The Secure Hash Algorithm, or SHA, is a family of encryption methods used in the creation and verification of digital signatures.

SHA is used to confirm the authenticity of documents and messages rather than encrypting the message itself. It is the underlying security standard used in the Internet security protocols TLS and SSL and is often used to verify Internet passwords.

The SHA standard was first introduced in 1993 and is an example of a cryptographic hash function that takes variable length text and condenses it to produce a message digest of a standard length. SHA's security is based on the presumption that from a given message digest it is unfeasible to work out the message that produced it or find two messages that produce the same message digest – known as a collision. Small changes to the input text also create significant changes in the digest.

The original SHA specification was withdrawn shortly after publication at the behest of the US National Security Agency because of a flaw in its design that reduced its security and was superseded in 1995 by SHA-1.

SHA-1 creates message digests that are 160 bits long. There are an infinite number of possible messages but only a limited number of possible message digests and the chance of discovering two messages that produce the same digest are 1 in 2^{80}. In 2005 a group of Chinese cryptanalysts announced that they had found a method that could find a possible collision faster than 2^{69} attempts. Although this is still a large number it was enough to sound the death knell for SHA-1 and in 2015, an attack was demonstrated for the first time.

The 256- or 512-bit SHA-2 issued in 2001 or the 1,600-bit SHA-3 announced in 2015 are now recommended instead of SHA-1. The NSA ordered government applications to use SHA-2 from 2010 while Google and Microsoft have said they will withdraw support for SHA-1 in 2017.

Using the cipher

To use SHA-1, you convert your message into a string of binary digits. In the ASCII notation system, for example, the letters A, B and C are represented by 01000001, 01000010 and 01000011 so the text ABC would be 010000010100001001000011, which has a message length of 24 digits.

We then create a padded message made up of the message in binary format at the start followed by the digit 1. At the end, we place the message length, expressed in 64-bit notation. Between these we place as many zeroes as required to make the padded message a multiple of 512 bits long

A padded message is divided into 512-bit blocks and these into 16 smaller 32-bit blocks or 'words' which are mathematically manipulated using a complex series of operations and functions as shown in the diagram right.

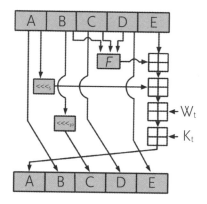

The boxes labelled A to E represent temporary 32-bit variables which have fixed values (set by the SHA-1 standard) at the beginning of the hashing process. This hashing process is carried out 80 times or iterations (indicated by the subscript letter t) for each 512-bit block with the new values of A to E fed back in at the top.

The boxes marked <<< represent a function which shifts the individual bits of what is input left by the indicated number of digits. The green box marked F represents one of five types of function that combines three 32-bit numbers to create a new 32-bit number.

The boxes marked with a plus indicate binary addition (in modulo 2^{32} arithmetic). K_t is a constant binary number that is specified in the SHA-1 standard. The 'words' – the 32-bit blocks of the actual message – are rolled into the algorithm where it is labelled W_t.

QUANTUM CRYPTOGRAPHY AND THE FUTURE

The odd world of quantum mechanics could prove to be the ultimate cryptographic method, although some experts have queried whether it will be of genuine practical use.

Measuring something seems like the easiest thing. Need the length of a piece of string? Just use a tape measure. Unfortunately, in the world of quantum mechanics, things go a little crazy because of something called the 'observer effect'. The problem is that, at some point, the things used for doing the measuring are on the same scale as the thing being measured and the act of measurement messes up what you are trying to do. It's like trying to measure tire pressure: hard to do without losing some air. Yet this very effect offers the possibility of a secure method of encryption, called quantum cryptography.

The photons that make up a beam of light vibrate in specific directions; this is known as their polarization and is the effect used in sunglasses that darken when it gets sunny. Light can be polarized in one of two ways: one in which vibration is horizontal or vertical (called rectilinear) and another in which vibration is diagonal. In quantum cryptography, these polarizations are used to represent the binary digits 0 and 1. For example, horizontal polarization (–) might represent a 0, making vertical polarization (|) represent 1. Or left-handed diagonal polarization (\) might be 0 and right-handed (/), 1. Quantum cryptography is at an early stage of development. In theory, the observer effect means that the system is unbreakable. However, as with other cryptographic systems, there is always the possibility of a man-in-the-middle attack, where the eavesdropper Eve impersonates Bob (see Public-key Encryption, pages 152-153).

Doubts about how important quantum cryptography might be centre not on the science, but on the question of whether it represents a genuine advance or is simply a more complex way of performing traditional and well-understood encryption methods. However, the system at the heart of it is as good as the laws of physics themselves. Quantum mechanics is one of the most accurate theories ever postulated. The numbers predicted by the equations of quantum electrodynamics, for example, agree with those found through experimental determination to within ten parts in a billion.

However, the history of science shows us that no theory is unassailable. When Sir Isaac Newton formulated his theory of gravity, science finally seemed to describe the perfection of the heavens – orbits, phases of the Moon, and eclipses could all be explained in a rigorous scientific manner. Yet, in 1915, Albert Einstein showed that while Newton was right, his law of gravitation was not, in fact, universal.

Quantum mechanics does not tell us everything about the world, and a deeper understanding of – for example – superstring theory may yet help us crack quantum cryptography. Then again, future advances in physics might also help us conceive new methods of encryption that are even harder to break.

Yet we may not even need to look so far ahead. Steganography, the ancient technique of concealing a message's existence rather than altering its letters or symbols, is making a comeback in the digital world (see pages 142–143.) Ever since the invention of the computer, the binary system has mounted a ferocious challenge to the dominance of the decimal system – so natural because of the ten digits on our hands. Yet, as we convert more and more of our information into binary digits – storing music, photographs, and text on computers and in the cloud, we have created the perfect environment for hiding messages among the huge strings of 0s and 1s that fill the world's servers. It is entirely possible to hide a message in the random fluctuations of an audio soundtrack or within the pixels of a photograph.

Welcome back to the future.

HOW TO BE A CRYPTANALYST

If you are an aspiring cryptanalyst, where should you start when presented with a message that was encrypted with an unknown cipher?

First of all, you should try to collect together as much encrypted material as possible, as a longer text can make all the difference. You should then analyze how many different symbols are used in the ciphertext. If there are only five or six characters (which could be letters, numbers or other symbols), then it is likely that a Polybius square (see page 24) or ADFGX cipher (see page 110) has been used.

After this, it is useful to try to establish the likely alphabet and language used, as this may tell us how many different symbols to expect in the ciphertext. Allied codebreakers at Bletchley Park knew that the material they were looking at was in German and Japanese; Middle Eastern cryptanalysts could guess that Arabic was the alphabet used. The Latin alphabet used in most of Europe and the West uses 26 letters while Cyrillic has 33, Arabic 28 and Greek 24. Of course the cryptologist may have used the same alphabet for the ciphertext as the plaintext but they may not.

Let us assume that the plaintext uses the 26-letter Latin alphabet. If the ciphertext is long and there are exactly 25 different symbols used then this may indicate the use of a Playfair cipher (see page 94). If there are more than 26 characters then this suggests that the method uses a nomenclator such as the Great Cipher (see page 70), homophonic substitution (see page 62) or a code rather than a cipher. If 26 ciphertext characters are present, we can look at the frequency of their appearance. Each language has a different average frequency of letter usage. In English, the letter Q appears with an average frequency of 0.14%. In French, this percentage is 1.06%, whereas the letter is almost never used in German. If you carry out a frequency analysis (see page 30) and look at the distribution charts, you can ascertain the most likely language to have been used. In English the most common letters are E, T, A, O and N while in French they are E, A, L, S and T; in German, E, N, I, R and S. You can similarly look at digraph and other n-gram analysis in English, the most common digraphs are TH, HE, AN, IN and ER while in French they are ES, EN, OU, DE and NT.

If the frequency distribution closely matches that of the expected language then it is likely that a substitution cipher has been used and working out the substitution used is a matter of replacing common letters and then guessing words. Short words or those containing punctuation are a good place to start. If the frequency distribution chart is flat then you can safely assume the cipher is polyalphabetic in nature and must turn to techniques such as the Kasiski method (page 122) and the index of coincidence (page 85) for help. For more complicated ciphers, you might have to rely on cribs, samples of known plaintext with the corresponding ciphertext that can be used to attack the cipher or code. For instance if a sender often sends similar sorts of message, such as weather reports for a location such as 'Spitzbergen,' then this can be used to identify how the plaintext has been encrypted. The computer age has given us the option of brute-force attacks in which we try every possible substitution or key. The computer can quickly step through every possibility and compare words in the decrypted message against text databases.

However, there is no guarantee that even the most determined cryptanalyst will succeed. In many cases, a lack of time or encrypted material will mean that cracking a cipher is simply impossible. Some of the unsolved puzzles and pieces of code in this book may thus remain forever unsolved, to tantalize codebreakers of the future and to inspire codemakers to continue with their endless quest for more complex and impenetrable methods of cryptography.

GLOSSARY

Alice: The generic name usually given to the sender of an encrypted message. See also Bob and Eve.

Asymmetric key: A system where different keys are used to encrypt and decrypt plaintext into ciphertext and vice versa.

Block cipher: A cipher which operates on a complete block of data rather than individual binary digits.

Bob: The generic name usually given to the recipient of an encrypted message. See also Alice and Eve.

Brute-force attack: An attempt to decrypt a code or cipher by trying every possible key in turn until the correct one is found.

Cipher: A method of hiding a message by transposing (scrambling) its letters or replacing each letter with another letter or symbol or groups of the same in a systematic way. Also referred to as encipherment.

Ciphertext: Text that has been encrypted. There is a convention that ciphertexts are written in uppercase letters. See also plaintext.

Code: An encryption system that uses a codebook of words or phrases with corresponding strings or text or numbers that are used to replace them. The sender and the recipient both typically require the same codebook.

Confusion: A property of a cipher that means that each binary digit of the ciphertext depends on several parts of the key.

Corpus: The entire body of ciphertexts in existence, particularly with reference to unbroken codes and alphabets.

Crib: A sample of known plaintext with its corresponding ciphertext that can be used to attack the cipher or code.

Cryptanalyst: A codebreaker.

Cryptogram: An encoded message that can be decrypted by simple methods, usually by hand, and often used for entertainment purposes. An example are the coded messages that appear in newspaper puzzle pages.

Depth: Two ciphertexts are said to be in depth when they have been encrypted using the same key. Using the same key can give a codebreaker a shortcut to decrypting a message.

Diffusion: A property of a cipher that means if a single bit of the plaintext is changed, at least half of the bits in the ciphertext should change.

Digraph: A group of two letters. Frequency analysis of digraphs can help in identifying correspondences between plaintext and ciphertext alphabets.

Eve: The generic name usually given to an eavesdropper wanting to intercept an encrypted message. See also Alice and Bob.

Fractionation: A cipher method that converts individual plaintext letters into several ciphertext symbols, for example by replacing letters for the X and Y coordinates of the plaintext letter in a cipher grid.

Frequency analysis: Counting the occurrences of symbols in a ciphertext and comparing them to the expected rate of occurrence of letters in a particular language in an attempt to identify particular correspondences.

Heuristic search: A technique that uses trial and error to make small changes in order to get closer to the solution and used as a shortcut to avoid an exhaustive search.

Hill climb: A type of iterative heuristic search where any putative solution is compared with the existing partial solution. Only those solutions that give better results are then adopted as the new partial solution.

Homophonic substitution: A system where more than one ciphertext character stands for each plaintext character with the object of securing against attack from frequency analysis.

Key: A piece of information, a word, phrase or series of binary digits for example, that specifies the transformation between plaintext and ciphertext.

Man-in-the-middle attack: Where an eavesdropper with malicious intent intercepts the communication between the sender and receiver and replaces the original message or key with one of their own without the knowledge of the other parties.

N-gram: A sequence of n contiguous symbols, syllables or words. An n-gram of length 2 is called a bigram, length 3 a trigram.

Null: Material, such as extra letters or words, added to a message to confuse the codebreaker, e.g. additional zeros added to the end of number-based ciphers.

Plaintext: Text that is to be encrypted. There is a convention used in cryptology that plaintexts are

written in lowercase letters. See also ciphertext. Also sometimes referred to as cleartext.

Polygraphic substitution cipher: A cipher in which groups of letters rather than individual ones are encrypted into other groups or symbols. They add extra security to the encryption by flattening the frequency distribution of groups of letters compared with individual ones. Larger amounts of ciphertext are also required for decryption.

Reciprocal cipher: A cipher whose encryption and decryption methods are the same.

Route cipher: A transposition cipher which uses a route through a grid of plaintext letters or words.

Steganography: Concealing a message, file or picture within another message, file or picture. The term combines the Greek words *steganos* (concealed) and *graphia* (writing).

Stream cipher: A cipher in which a binary digit from the plaintext is combined with a digit from a stream of pseudorandom binary digits (keystream) to produce a binary digit in the ciphertext.

Substitution cipher: A cipher in which letters in the plaintext are replaced by other letters or groups of letters See also Transposition cipher.

Symmetric key: A key which is used for both the encryption and decryption processes.

Transposition cipher: A cipher in which the letters in the plaintext are rearranged, often in a complex manner. An anagram is a simple example. See also Substitution cipher.

BIBLIOGRAPHY

Alberti , L.B. (tr. Zaccagnini, A.) (1997). De Cifris, *A Treatise on Ciphers* (1467). Galimberti. Torino.

Bauer, F.L. (1991). *Decrypted Secrets: Methods and Maxims of Cryptology*. Springer.

Bazeries, E. (1901). Les Chiffres Secrets Dévoilés. Paris: E. Fasquelle.

Bellaso, G.B. (1553). *La cifra del Sig. Giovan Battista Bel[l]aso, gentil'huomo bresciano, nuovamente da lui medesimo ridotta à grandissima brevità et perfettione*. Venetia.

Bellaso, G.B. (1564). *Il vero modo di scrivere in cifra con facilita, prestezza et securezza*. Bressa: Jacobo Britanico.

Bennett, C.H. IBM Research & Brassard, G. *Quantum Cryptography Public Key Distribution and Coin Tossing*, Montreal: University of Montreal.

Bertrand, G. (1973). *Enigma ou la plus grande énigme de la guerre 1939–1945*, Paris, Librairie Plon.

Bolton, Sir F.J. (1871). Bolton's Telegraph Code, *A Telegraphic Dictionary of the English Language*. London: Longmans, Green, Reader & Dyer.

Bould, M. & Reid, M. (eds) (2005). *Parietal Games*. Cambridge: Science Fiction Foundation.

Bowers B. (2001). *Sir Charles Wheatstone FRS: 1802-1875, History of Technology series 29*, London: IEE.

Brann N. L. (1981). *The Abbott Trithemius (1462–1516),The Renaissance of Monastic Humanism*. Leiden: Brill.

Brooks, P.G.Q. *The Dorabella Cipher: intro, Effluvium of Consciousness* blog. baldfatgit. files.wordpress.com /2010/02/14/the-dorabella-cipher-intro/

Brumbaugh, R.S. (1978). *The World's Most Mysterious Manuscript*. Carbondale: Southern Illinois University Press.

Buckland M. K. (2006). *Emanuel Goldberg and His Knowledge Machine*. Greenwood Publishing.

Byrne, J.F. (1953). *Silent Years: An Autobiography with Memoirs of James Joyce and Our Ireland*. New York: Farrar, Straus & Young.

Calder G. (1917). *Auraicept na n-éces: the scholars' primer; being the texts of the Ogham tract from the Book of Ballymote and the Yellow book of Lecan, and the text of the Trefhocul from the Book of Leinster*. Edinburgh: John Grant.

Candela, R. (1938). *The Military Cipher of Commandant Bazeries*. New York: Cardanus Press.

Cardano, G. Schmidt, J. (tr.) (2002). *De vita propria liber*, New York Review Books.

Carter, F. & Gallehawk, J. (1998), *The Enigma Machine and the Bombe. The Story of the Breaking of the Enigma Cipher over the Period 1932-1945*. The Bletchley Park Trust Reports, No. 9.

Communications Instructions Operating Signals (2009). Combined Communications Electronics Board.

Cowan, M.J. *Chaocipher: Solving exhibits 1 and 4*. www.cryptoden.com

Cryptologic Almanac 50th Anniversary Series. Madame X: Agnes Meyer Driscoll and U.S. Naval Cryptology, 1919–1940, NSA.

d'Agapeyeff, A. (1939). *Codes and Ciphers*. Oxford: Oxford University Press.

de Vigenère, B. (1586). *Traicté des chiffres, ou secrètes manières d'escrire*. Paris.

Desfemmes, General A. (1974). 'Reflexions sur la guerre éléctronique,' *La Jaune et La Rouge*, July/August 1974.

Dhavare, A., Low, R.M., Stamp, M. *Efficient Cryptanalysis of Homophonic Substitution Ciphers*. San Jose State University. www.cs.sjsu.edu/faculty/stamp/RUA/homophonic.pdf.

D'Imperio, M.E. (1978). *The Voynich Manuscript: An Elegant Enigma*, National Security Agency.

Eisenberg, Dr J. M. (2008). 'The Phaistos Disk: A One-Hundred-Year old Hoax?,' *Minerva*, July/August, pp 9–24.

Enoksen, L.M. (1998). *Runor: historia, tydning, tolkning*. Falun: Historiska Media.

Evans, A. (1952). *Scripta Minoa: The Written Documents of Minoan Crete: with Special Reference to the Archives of Knossos*. Oxford: Clarendon Press.

Federal Bureau of Investigation. *The Hollow Nickel Case*. www.fbi.gov/history/ famous-cases/hollow-nickel-rudolph-abel

Ferguson, N., Schneier, B., & Kohno, T. (2010). *Cryptography Engineering, Design Principles and Practical Applciations*. Indianapolis: Wiley Publishing.

Franksen, O.I. (1985). *Mr. Babbage's Secret: the Tale of a Cipher – and APL*. Prentice Hall.

Franksen, O.I. (1991). *Babbage and Cryptography, Or the Mystery of Admiral Beaufort's Cipher*, Technical University of Denmark, lecture at the Babbage-Faraday Bicenteary Conference, 5–7 July 1991.

Friedman, W.F. (1922). *The Index of Coincidence and its applications in cryptanalysis*. New York: Aegean Park Press.

Friedman, W.F. (1942). *American Army Field Codes in the American Expeditionary Forces During the First World War*. US Government Printing Office.

Friendly, A. (1977). *Beaufort of the Admiralty. The Life of Sir Francis Beaufort, 1774-1857*. New York: Random House.

Gaines, H.F. (1939). *Elementary Cryptanalysis: A Study of Ciphers and Their Solution*. London: Chapman and Hall.

Hahalruna and El-Mushajjar, *The Grey Book of Runes*, 22 January 2012, http:// greybookofrunes.blogspot.co.uk/

Herodotus (tr. Rawlinson, G. and. Macaulay, G. C.) (1932). *The Histories*. New York, Tudor Pub. Co.

Hill, L.S. (1929). 'Cryptography in an Algebraic Alphabet,' *American Mathematics Monthly*, vol 36, no 6, June/July 1929

International Radio Telegraph Convention of Berlin: 1906 and Propositions for the International Radio Telegraph Conference of London. Washington: Government Printing Office, (1912.)

Jakobsen, T. (1995) *A Fast Method for the Cryptanalysis of Substitution Ciphers*. *Cryptologia*, Volume 19 Number 3 October 1995, pp. 265-274.

Johnson, K.W. (2015). *The Neglected Giant: Agnes Meyer Driscoll*, NSA Center for Cryptologic History.

Joyner, D. (2013). *Elizabeth Smith Friedman, up to 1934*. http://www. wdjoyner.com/papers/elizabeth-friedman_ early-crypto-work4.pdf.

Kahn, D. (1996). *The Codebreakers: The Comprehensive History of Secret Communication from Ancient Times to the Internet* (Rev sub ed.)New York: Scribner.

Kapera, Z.J. (1990). *Marian Rejewski, The Man who Defeated Enigma*. The Enigma Press, Krakow.

Kasiski, F. W. (1863). *Die Geheimschriften und die Dechiffrir-Kunst*. Berlin: E. S. Mittler und Sohn.

Kaulis, A. (2008). *The Phaistos Disk: An Ancient Enigma Solved*, International Conference on the Phaistos Disk.

Kerckhoffs, A. (1883). 'La cryptographie militaire,' *Journal des sciences militaires*, vol. IX, pp. 5–38, Janvier 1883, pp. 161–191, Février 1883.

King, D.A. (2001). *The Ciphers of the Monks: A Forgotten Number-notation of the Middle Ages*. Stuttgart: F. Steiner.

Knight, K., Megyesi, B., & Schaefer, C. (2011). *The Copiale Cipher*, Proceedings of the 4th Workshop on Building and Using Comparable Corpora, pages 2–9, 49th Annual Meeting of the Association for Computational Linguistics.

Kvittingen, I. (2014), Mysterious code in Viking runes is cracked, *ScienceNordic*, 5 February 2014.

Laville, S. 'Bletchley veterans tackle "toughest puzzle yet". *Guardian*, 12 May 2004.

Leigh, R., Baigent, M. and Lincoln, H. (1982), *The Holy Blood and The Holy Grail*. London: Jonathan Cape.

Maffeo, Capt S.E. *U.S. Navy Codebreakers, Linguists, and Intelligence Officers against Japan 1910–1941: A Biographical Dictionary.* London: Rowman and Littlefield Publishers.

Marks, L. (1998). *Between Silk and Cyanide: A Codemaker's Story 1941–1945.* London: HarperCollins.

Matossian, M.K., *The Phaistos Disk: A Solar Calendar. Contribution To A Decipherment, Mediterranean Archaeology and Archaeometry,* Vol. 13, No 1, pp.235–264.

Miller, F.(1882), *Telegraphic Code to Insure Privacy and Secrecy in the Transmission of Telegrams,* New York: CM Cornwell.

Mohammad Mrayati (ed), Said M al-Asaad (tr), *Arabic Origins of Cryptology,* series 3, ibn ad Durayhim's Treatise on Cryptanalysis. KFCRIS/KACST.

Morris, S. 'Has the mystery of the Holy Grail been solved?' *Guardian*, 26 November 2004

Morse, S.F.B. (1840). *Improvement in the Mode of Communication Information by Signals by the Application of Electro-Magnetism.* US Patent 1647.

Mucklow, T.J. (2015). *The SIGABA / ECM II Cipher Machine : A Beautiful Idea.* Fort Meade: National Security Agency, Center for Cryptologic History.

Packard, W.E. (2009). 'Morse Code: Efficient or Over the Hill?' *QST*, January.

Palmer, J. (aka Gaffney, T.) (2006). *The Agony Column Codes and Ciphers*, Authors Online Ltd,.

Parpola A (2005). *Study of the Indus Script.* Session of the International Conference of Eastern Studies.

Pelling, N. (2013). *The d'Agapeyeff Cipher once again . . .* Ciphermysteries.com, 23 December 2013.

Plutarch. *The Parallel Lives*, Vol IV. Loeb Classical Library.

Polybius. Robyn Waterfield (tr. 2010) *The Histories.* Oxford: Oxford University Press.

Powell, Mrs R. (Dora Penny) (1937), *Edward Elgar: Memories of a Variation.* London: Oxford University Press.

Procedures for Air Navigation Services: Abbreviations and Codes, ICAO Doc 8400, eighth edition 2010.

Reid, J.D. (1879), *The Telegraph in America,* New York: Derby Brothers.

Rivest, R., Shamir, A., & Adleman, L. (1978), *A Method for Obtaining Digital Signatures and Public-Key Cryptosystems.* Communications of the ACM, Vol. 21 (2), 1978, pp.120–126.

Roberts, T.S., *Solving the Dorabella Cipher.* http://unsolvedproblems.org

Rosenheim, S.J. (1997), *The Cryptographic Imagination: Secret Writing from Edgar Poe to the Internet.* Baltimore: Johns Hopkins University Press.

Rubin, M. *Chaocipher revealed.* http://www.mountainvistasoft.com/chaocipher/ActualChaocipher/Chaocipher-Revealed-Algorithm.pdf

Sale, T. *The Lorenz Cipher and how Bletchley Park broke it.* www.codesandciphers.org.

Sams, E. (1970), *Elgar's Cipher Letter to Dorabella*, The Musical Times, Vol. 111, No. 1524 February, pp. 151–154.

Sams, E. (1970). *Variations on an Original Theme (Enigma).* The Musical Times, March, pp 258–262.

Sayers, D.L. (1932). *Have His Carcase.* London: Victor Gollancz.

Shannon, C. (1996). *Communication Theory of Secrecy Systems.* Bell System Technical Journal 28 (4), pp 656–715.

The Friedman Legacy. A tribute to William and Elizebeth Friedman. Sources in Cryptologic History Number 3. National Security Agency, 2006.

Tranquillus G. S. James Rives (ed. 2007) *The Lives of the Twelve Caesars.* London: Penguin.

Unicode: The Universal Telegraphic Phrase-book: A Code of Cypher Words for Commercial, Domestic and Familiar Phrases in Ordinary Use in Inland and Foreign Telegrams (1889). London: Casell & Company.

Ventris, M. and Chadwick, J. (1953), 'Evidence for Greek Dialect in the Mycenaean Archives', *The Journal of Hellenic Studies*, Vol. 73, pp. 84–103.

Vovnich, W.M. (1921), 'A Preliminary Sketch of the History of the Roger Bacon Cipher Manuscript'. *Transactions of the College of Physicians of Philadelphia*, pp. 415–430.

Wiesner, S. (1983), *Conjugate Coding.* SIGACT News 15:1, 78–88.

Williams, K., March, L.and Wassell, S.R. (2010), *The Mathematical Works of Leon Battista Alberti.* Basel: Springer.

Yardley, H.O. (1929), *The American Black Chamber.* Indianapolis: Bobbs-Merrill.

USEFUL WEB LINKS

Analyze text for ngrams:
www.guidetodatamining.com/ngramAnalyzer/

Frequency analysis tool:
www.characterfrequencyanalyzer.com/

Forum on uncracked historical ciphers:
www.ciphermysteries.com

Database of commercial codebooks:
www.dtc.umn.edu/~reedsj/codebooks.txt

Cryptographer Elonka Dunin, including list of unsolved codes and ciphers:
http://elonka.com/

Crypto Corner, details of all the major codes:
http://crypto.interactive-maths.com/

Emulator of Japan's wartime Purple machine
http://cryptocellar.org/simula/purple/index.html

Blog on mathematics and cryptography:
www.jimblog.net

International Association for Cryptologic Research:
www.iacr.org

National Security Agency:
www.nsa.gov

National Cryptologic Museum:
www.nsa.gov/about/cryptologic_heritage/museum/

Government Communications Headquarters:
www.gchq.gov.uk

Bletchley Park Trust:
www.bletchleypark.org.uk

Online Enigma machine challenges:
http://turinggame.sciencemuseum.org.uk/

Vectors site with a detailed history of cryptography:
www.vectorsite.net/ttcode.html

CIA code challenges:
www.cia.gov/kids-page/games/break-the-code

Open source cryptography tools:
www.cryptool.org

Index

AUTHOR ACKNOWLEDGEMENTS

I would like to thank Clare, Lola, Seth and Reuben for letting me write when I really should be with them and my parents for being super-efficient publicity machines for my books. And finally to all the people, past and present, of Bletchley Park who continue to inspire me with their dedication.

Picture Credits